A SERIOUS MAN

A SERIOUS MAN

Ethan Coen and Joel Coen

faber and faber

First published in 2009
by Faber and Faber Limited
74–77 Great Russell Street, London WC1B 3DA
Published in the United States by Faber and Faber Inc.
an affiliate of Farrar, Straus and Giroux LLC, New York

Typeset by Country Setting, Kingsdown, Kent CT14 8ES
Printed in England by CPI Bookmarque, Croydon, Surrey

A CIP record for this book
is available from the British Library

ISBN 978-0-571-25532-0

2 4 6 8 10 9 7 5 3 1

A Serious Man

White letters on a black screen:

RECEIVE WITH SIMPLICITY
EVERYTHING THAT HAPPENS TO YOU
Rashi

Fade in:

SNOWFLAKES FALLING IN BLACK

The flakes drift lazily down toward us. Our angle looks straight up.

Now an angle looking steeply down: the snow falls not quite dead away to collect on a foreground chimney pot and on the little shtetl street that lies maplike below us.

It is night, and quiet, and the street is deserted except for one man who walks away from us, his valenki *squeaking in the fresh snow. He leads a horse and cart.*

We cut down to street level. The man walks toward us, bearded, and bundled against the cold. Smiling, he mutters in Yiddish – the dialogue subtitled.

MAN
What a marvel . . . what a marvel . . .

HOUSE INTERIOR

The man enters.

MAN
Dora!

VOICE
Yes . . .

The man crosses to the stove with a bundle of wood. Dora's voice continues:

. . . Can you help me with the ice?

3

The man dumps the wood into a box by the stove as his wife enters with an ice pick.

. . . I expected you hours ago.

MAN

You can't imagine what just happened. I was coming back on the Lublin road when the wheel came off the cart – thank heavens it was the way back and I'd already sold the geese!

WIFE

How much?

MAN

Fifteen groshen, but that's not the story. I was struggling to set the cart upright when a droshky approaches from the direction of Lvov. How lucky, you think, that someone is out this late.

WIFE

Yes, very remarkable.

MAN

But that's the least of it! He stops to help me; we talk of this, we talk of that – it turns out this is someone you know! Traitle Groshkover!

His wife stares at him as he beams. He takes the stare as a sign that she can't place the name.

. . . You know, Reb Groshkover! Pesel Bunim's uncle! The *chacham* from Lodz, who studied under the Zohar reb in Krakow!

Still she stares. Then, quietly:

WIFE

God has cursed us.

MAN

What?

WIFE

Traitle Groshkover has been dead for three years.

4

Laughter erupts from the man but, as his wife continues to stare at him, he strangles on it.

Quiet.

Wind whistles under the eaves.

The man says quietly:

> MAN
> Why do you say such a thing! I saw the man! I talked to him!

> WIFE
> You talked to a dybbuk. Traitle Groshkover died of typhus in Pesel Bunim's house. Pesel told me – she sat *shiva* for him.

They stare at each other. Outside, the wind quickens.

A rap at the door.

Neither husband nor wife immediately respond.

Finally, to her husband:

> WIFE
> . . . Who is it?

> MAN
> I . . . invited him here. For some soup, to warm himself.

The wind moans.

> . . . He helped me, Dora!

THE DOOR

We are looking in from the outside as the door unlatches and creaks in, opened by the husband in the foreground, who has arranged his face into a strained look of greeting. In the background the wife stares, hollow-eyed.

> MAN
> Reb Groshkover! You are welcome here!

*Reverse on Reb Groshkover: a short, merry-looking fellow with a
bifurcated beard. He gives a little squeal of delight.*

REB GROSHKOVER

You are too kind, Velvel! Too kind!

He steps into the house and sees the wife staring at him.

. . . And you must be Dora! So much I have heard of you!
Yes, your cheeks are pink and your legs are stout! What a
wife you have!

The husband chuckles nervously.

MAN

Yes! A ray of sun, a ray of sun! Sit!

WIFE

My husband said he offered you soup.

REB GROSHKOVER

Yes, but I couldn't possibly eat this late, or I'd have
nightmares. No, no: no soup for me!

WIFE

I knew it.

Reb Groshkover laughs.

REB GROSHKOVER

I see! You think I'm fat enough already!

He settles, chuckling, into his chair, but Dora remains sober.

WIFE

No. A dybbuk doesn't eat.

Reb Groshkover stares at her, shocked.

The wife holds his look, giving no ground.

The husband looks from wife to Reb Groshkover, apprehensive.

A heavy silence.

Reb Groshkover bursts into pealing laughter.

REB GROSHKOVER

What a wife you have!

6

He wipes away tears of merriment; the husband relaxes, even begins to smile.

> MAN
>
> I assure you, Reb Groshkover, it's nothing personal; she heard a story you had died, three years ago, at Pesel Bunim's house. This is why she thinks you are a dybbuk; I, of course, do not believe in such things. I am a rational man.

Reb Groshkover is still chuckling.

> REB GROSHKOVER
>
> Oh my. Oh my yes. What nonsense. And even if there were spirits, certainly . . .

He thumps his chest.

> . . . I am not one of them!

> WIFE
>
> Pesel always worried. Your corpse was left unattended for many minutes when Pesel's father broke *shmira* and left the room – it must have been then that the Evil One –

She breaks off to spit at the mention of the Evil One.

> – took you!

Reb Groshkover is terribly amused:

> REB GROSHKOVER
>
> "My corpse!" Honestly! What a wife you have!

> WIFE
>
> Oh yes? Look, husband . . .

She steps forward to the reb, who looks enquiringly up at her.

> . . . They were preparing the body. Pesel's father shaved one cheek . . .

As his eyes roll down to look at her hand, she draws it across his smooth right cheek.

> . . . Then he left the room. He came back, and shaved the other . . .

7

She reaches across to the other cheek, Reb Groshkover's eyes following her hand –

   . . . You were already gone!

– and drags her fingers across. A bristly sound.

Reb Groshkover laughs.

> REB GROSHKOVER
> I shaved hastily this morning and missed a bit – by you this makes me a dybbuk?

He appeals to the husband:

   . . . It's true, I was sick with typhus when I stayed with Pesel, but I recovered, as you can plainly see, and now I – hungh!

The wife steps back.

Reb Groshkover looks slowly down at his own chest in which the wife has just planted an ice pick.

Reb Groshkover stares at the ice pick.

The wife stares.

The husband stares.

Reb Groshkover bursts out laughing:

   . . . What a wife you have!

The husband can manage only a shocked whisper:

> MAN
> Woman, what have you done?

Reb Groshkover looks down again at the ice pick in his chest, the sight refreshing his laughter. He shakes his head.

> REB GROSHKOVER
> Yes, what have you done?

He looks at the husband.

   . . . I ask you, Velvel, as a rational man: which of us is possessed?

WIFE

What do you say now about spirits? He is unharmed!

REB GROSHKOVER

On the contrary! I don't feel at all well.

And indeed, blood has begun to soak through his vest.

He chuckles with less energy.

. . . One does a mitzvah and this is the thanks one gets?

MAN

Dora! Woe, woe! How can such a thing be!

REB GROSHKOVER

Perhaps I *will* have some soup. I am feeling weak . . .

He rises to his feet but totters.

. . . Or perhaps I should go . . .

He smiles weakly at Dora.

. . . One knows when one isn't wanted.

He walks unsteadily to the door, opens it with effort, and staggers out into the moaning wind and snow to be swallowed by the night.

The wife and husband stare at the door banging in the wind.

Finally:

MAN

Dear wife. We are ruined. Tomorrow they will discover the body. All is lost.

WIFE

Nonsense, Velvel.

She walks to the door . . .

Blessed is the Lord. Good riddance to evil.

. . . and shuts it against the wind.

BLACK

A drumbeat thumps in black.

Music: Jefferson Airplane. Grace Slick's voice enters:

> "When the truth is found to be lies
> And all the joy within you dies
> Don't you want somebody to love . . ."

An image fades in slowly, but even full up it is dim: a round, dull white shape with a black pinhole center. This white half-globe is a plug set in a flesh-toned field. The flesh tone glows translucently, backlit. We are drifting toward the white plug and, as we do so, the music grows louder still.

AN EARPIECE

A pull back – a reverse of the preceding push in – from the white plastic earpiece of a transistor radio. The Jefferson Airplane continues over the cut but becomes extremely compressed. The pull back reveals that the earpiece, lodged in someone's ear, trails a white cord.

We drift down the cord to find the radio at its other end. As we do so we hear, live in the room, many voices speaking a foreign language in unison. A classroom, apparently.

The radio, on a desktop, is hidden from in front by a book held open before it. The book is written in non-Roman characters.

We are in Hebrew school.

The boy who is listening to the transistor radio – Danny Gopnik – sits at a hinge-topped desk in a cinderblock classroom whose rows of desks are occupied by other boys and girls of about twelve years of age. It is dusk and the room is fluorescent-lit.

At the front of the room an elderly teacher performs a soporific verb conjugation.

Danny straightens one leg so that he may dig into a pocket. With an eye on the teacher to make sure he isn't being watched, he eases something out:

A twenty-dollar bill.

TEACHER
Mee yodayah? Reuven? Rifkah? Mah zeh, "anakim"?

BLINDING LIGHT

The light resolves into a flared image of a blinking eye.

Reverse: the inside of a human ear – fleshy whorls finely veined, a cavity receding to dark.

Objective on the doctor's office: the doctor is peering through a lightscope into the ear of an early-middle-aged man, Larry Gopnik.

DOCTOR
Uh-huh.

HEBREW SCHOOL

Close on Hebrew characters being scribbled onto the blackboard as the teacher talks.

The teacher, talking.

A bored child, staring off.

His point-of-view: a blacktopped parking lot with a few orange school buses; beyond it a marshy field and distant suburban tract housing.

Close on another child staring through drooping eyelids.

His point-of-view: very close on the face of a classroom clock. We hear its electrical hum. Its red sweep second hand crawls around the dial very, very slowly.

Danny Gopnik hisses:

DANNY
Fagle! . . .

The teacher drones on, writing on the blackboard. Danny's eyes flit from the teacher to the student sitting kitty-corner in front of him – a husky youth with shaggy hair. He hasn't heard Danny.

. . . Fagle!

The teacher turns from the blackboard and Danny leans back, eyes front, folding the twenty up small behind his book.

The teacher, not finding the source of the noise, turns back to the board and resumes the droning lesson.

The clock-watching child, eyelids sinking, is beginning to drool out of one side of his mouth.

DOCTOR'S OFFICE

The light again flares.

Reverse: looking into a pupil.

Objective: the doctor looking through his scope into Larry's eye.

DOCTOR

Mm-hmm.

HEBREW SCHOOL

The teacher drones on at the blackboard.

A bored child excavates a booger from his nose.

DANNY

Fagle!

The teacher interrupts himself briefly to make a couple of phlegm-hawking sounds, then resumes.

DOCTOR'S OFFICE

The doctor palpates Larry's midriff, digging his fingers into the hairy, baggy flesh.

DOCTOR'S VOICE

Uh-huh. We'll do some routine X-rays.

HEBREW SCHOOL

A young girl holds a hank of her bangs in front of her face, separating out individual hairs to examine them for split ends.

The teacher turns from the board and begins to pace the desk aisles, looking back and forth among the students, posing questions.

The booger-seeker, having successfully withdrawn a specimen, drapes it carefully over the sharp end of his pencil, to what end we cannot know.

Danny, apprehensively eyeing the teacher, slides the twenty into the transistor radio's cover-sleeve.

X-RAY CONE

A huge white rubberized cone, pointed directly at us.

We hear a rush of static and the doctor's voice filtered through a talk-back:

DOCTOR'S VOICE

Hold still.

Wider: Larry is in his shorts lying on his back on an examining table that is covered by a sheet of tissue paper. The X-ray cone is pointed at the middle of his body.

There is a brief sci-fi-like machine hum. It clicks off.

HEBREW SCHOOL

The clock-watching student's head is bobbing slowly toward his chest.

The teacher's circuit of the classroom has taken him around behind Danny. Danny's book lies face-down on the desk, covering the radio, but the white cord snakes out from under it up to his ear. The teacher's questions and perambulation stop short as he notices the cord.

TEACHER

Mah zeh?

He yanks at the cord.

The cord pops out of its jack and Jefferson Airplane blares tinnily from beneath the book of Torah stories.

The teacher lifts the book to expose the jangling radio.

Outraged, the teacher projects above the music:

. . . Mah zeh?! Mah zeh?!

Some of the students sing along with the music; some beat rhythm on their desks.

. . . Sheket, talmidim! Sheket bivakasha!

Three students join in a chorus:

STUDENTS

Sheket! Sheket bivakasha!

The nodding student's head droops ever lower.

Other students join in the chant:

CHORUS

SHAH! SHAH! SHEKET BIVAKASHA!

The nodding student's chin finally reaches, and settles upon, his chest as a long clattering inhale signals his surrender to sleep.

DOCTOR'S OFFICE

Larry, now fully clothed, is seated across from the doctor.

The doctor examines his file. He absently taps a cigarette out of a pack and lights up. He nods as he smokes, looking at the file.

DOCTOR

Well, I – sorry.

He holds the pack toward Larry.

LARRY

No thanks.

DOCTOR

Well, you're in good health. How're Judith and the kids?

LARRY

Good. Everyone's good. You know.

The doctor takes a long suck.

DOCTOR

Good. Daniel must be – what? About to be bar mitzvah?

LARRY

Two weeks.

DOCTOR

Well, mazel tov. They grow up fast, don't they?

TINTED PHOTO PORTRAIT

The portrait, old, in an ornate gilt frame, is of a middle-aged rabbi with a small neat moustache and round spectacles. He wears a tallis hood-style and has a phylactery box strapped to his forehead. A plaque set into the picture frame identifies the man as Rabbi Marshak.

Wider shows that the portrait hangs in the Hebrew school principal's office, a white cinderblock room. It is quiet. The only sound is a deep electrical hum.

Just visible behind the principal's desk, upon which is a low stack of books and a name plate identifying the occupant as MAR TURCHIK, is the top of a man's head – an old man, with a few wispy white hairs where his yarmulka is not.

Danny, seated opposite, pushes up from his slouch to better see across the desk.

We boom up to show more of the principal. He is short. He wears a white shirt and hoist-up pants that come to just below his armpits. He has thick eyeglasses. He fiddles with the transistor radio, muttering:

PRINCIPAL

Hmm . . . eh . . . nu?

He experiments with different dials on the radio.

DANNY

You put the –

The old man holds up one hand.

PRINCIPAL

B'ivrit.

DANNY

Um . . .

The old man looks down at the little earpiece pinched between two fingers. He examines the contrivance like a superstitious native handling an unfamiliar fetish.

We cut to the source of the electrical hum: a wall clock whose red sweep second hand crawls around the dial very, very slowly.

The reb continues to squint at the earpiece.

Danny sighs. He encourages:

DANNY

Yeah, you –

The principal's tone is harder:

PRINCIPAL

B'ivrit.

This time his cold look holds until he is sure that the admonishment has registered.

He looks back down at the earpiece.

The door opens, ignored by the principal, and an old woman shuffles in with a teacup chattering on a saucer. She has thick eyeglasses. She wears thick flesh-colored support hose. She takes slow, short steps toward the desk. The principal continues studying the radio.

PRINCIPAL

Mneh . . .

The old woman's gait makes for slow progress and a continuously rattling teacup. She bears on toward the principal. The tableau looks like a performance-art piece.

She reaches the desk and sets the teacup down. She summons a couple of phlegm-hawking rasps and turns.

She takes slow short steps toward the door.

The principal raises the earpiece experimentally toward his ear.

Close on his hairy, wrinkled ear as his trembling fingers bring in the earpiece. The fingers push and wobble and tamp the earpiece into place, hesitate, and then do some more pushing and wobbling and tamping.

The principal keeps Danny fixed with a stare as his hand hesitantly drops from his ear, ready to reach back up should the earpiece do anything tricky.

. . . mneh . . .

Satisfied that neither the student nor the earpiece are about to make any sudden moves, he looks down at the radio. He turns a dial.

Issuing faintly from the imperfectly lodged earpiece is the tinny jangle of rock and roll. The rabbi stares blankly, listening.

Danny waits.

The rabbi is expressionless, mouth slightly open, listening.

Tableau: anxious student, earplugged spiritual leader.

Muffled, from the outer office, the hawking of phlegm.

CLASSROOM

We are behind a man who writes equations on a chalkboard, shoulder at work and hand quickly waggling. Periodically he glances back, giving us a fleeting look at his face: it is Larry Gopnik.

LARRY
You following this? . . . Okay? . . . So . . . Heh-heh . . . This part is exciting . . .

Students watch, bored.

. . . So, okay. So. So if that's that, then we can do this, right? Is that right? Isn't that right? And that's Schrödinger's paradox, right? Is the cat dead or is the cat not dead? Okay?

BLEGEN HALL

Larry enters the physics department office. The department's secretary wheels her castored chair away from her typing.

SECRETARY
Messages, Professor Gopnik.

He takes the three phone messages.

LARRY
Thank you, Natalie. Oh – Clive. Come in.

A waiting Korean graduate student rises from his outer-office chair.

LARRY'S OFFICE

Larry flips through the messages. Absently:

> LARRY
> . . . So, uh, what can I do for you?

The messages:

> WHILE YOU WERE OUT *Dick Dutton of Columbia Record Club*
> CALLED REGARDING: *"Please call."*

> WHILE YOU WERE OUT *Sy Ableman*
> CALLED REGARDING: *"Let's talk."*

> WHILE YOU WERE OUT *Clive Park*
> CALLED REGARDING: *"Unjust test results."*

He crumples the last one.

> CLIVE
> Uh, Dr. Gopnik, I believe the results of physics mid-term were unjust.

> LARRY
> Uh-huh, how so?

> CLIVE
> I received an unsatisfactory grade. In fact: F, the failing grade.

> LARRY
> Uh, yes. You failed the mid-term. That's accurate.

> CLIVE
> Yes, but this is not just. I was unaware to be examined on the mathematics.

> LARRY
> Well – you can't do physics without mathematics, really, can you?

> CLIVE
> If I receive failing grade I lose my scholarship, and feel shame. I understand the physics. I understand the dead cat.

LARRY
(*surprised*)
You understand the dead cat?

Clive nods gravely.

But . . . you . . . you can't really understand the physics
without understanding the math. The math tells how it
really works. That's the real thing; the stories I give you in
class are just illustrative; they're like, fables, say, to help give
you a picture. An imperfect model. I mean – even I don't
understand the dead cat. The math is how it really works.

Clive shakes his head, dubious.

CLIVE
Very difficult . . . very difficult . . .

LARRY
Well, I . . . I'm sorry, but I . . . what do you propose?

CLIVE
Passing grade.

LARRY
No no, I –

CLIVE
Or perhaps I can take the mid-term again. Now I know it
covers mathematics.

LARRY
Well, the other students wouldn't like that, would they.
If one student gets to retake the test till he gets a grade he
likes.

Clive impassively considers this.

CLIVE
Secret test.

LARRY
No, I'm afraid –

CLIVE
Hush-hush.

No, that's just not workable. I'm afraid we'll just have to bite the bullet on this thing, Clive, and –

CLIVE

Very troubling.

He rises.

   . . . very troubling . . .

He goes to the door, shaking his head, and Larry watches his unexcused exit in surprise.

Larry stares at the open door. The secretary outside, her back to us, types on.

Larry looks stupidly around his own office, then shakes his head.

He picks up the phone message from Sy Ableman – "Let's talk" – and dials. As he dials, his other hand wanders over the papers on his desktop.

There is a plain white envelope on the desk. Larry picks it up as the phone rings through. A ring is clipped short and a warm basso-baritone rumbles through the line:

PHONE VOICE

Sy Ableman.

LARRY

Hello, Sy, Larry Gopnik.

SY
(*mournful*)
Larry. How are you, my friend?

Larry picks idly at the envelope.

LARRY

Good, how've you been, Sy?

Inside the envelope: a thick sheaf of one-hundred-dollar bills.

SY

Oh fine. Shall we talk, Larry?

Larry reacts to the money.

LARRY
(*into phone*)
What?! Oh! Sorry! I, uh – call back!

He slams down the phone.

   . . . Clive!

He rushes out the door, through the secretarial area and into the hallway.

Empty.

He looks at the stuffed envelope he still holds.

He goes back to the departmental office. The secretary sits typing. She glances at him and, as she goes back to her typing:

SECRETARY
Sy Ableman just called. Said he got disconnected.

BATHROOM DOOR

A hand enters to knock.

MAN'S VOICE
Out in a minute!

Sarah, the sixteen-year-old girl who has just knocked, rolls her eyes.

SARAH
I gotta wash my hair! I'm going out tonight!

VOICE
Out in a minute!

SARAH
Jesus Christ!

She stomps down the hall.

KITCHEN

Judith, a woman of early middle age, is at the stove. Sarah enters.

SARAH

Why is Uncle Arthur *always* in the bathroom?

JUDITH

He has to drain his sebaceous cyst. You know that. Will you set the table?

SARAH

Why can't he do it in the basement? Or go out in the garage!

BUS

We are raking the exterior of an orange school bus as it rattles along. Hebrew characters on the side identify it – to some, anyway.

INSIDE

We are locked down on Danny as the bus rattles like an old crate, squeaking, grinding gears, belching exhaust. Danny and the children around him vibrate and pitch about without reaction, accustomed to it.

They raise their voices over the engine and the various stress noises in the chassis as well as a transistor radio somewhere that plays Jefferson Airplane.

DANNY

I had twenty bucks in it too. Inside the case.

RONNIE NUDELL

Twenty bucks! How come?

DANNY

I bought a lid from Mike Fagle. Couple weeks ago. I still owed him twenty.

RONNIE NUDELL

He already gave you the pot?

DANNY

Yeah, but a couple weeks ago my funding got cut off. Fagle said he'd pound the crap out of me if I didn't pay up.

HOWARD ALTAR

What funding got cut off? Where do you get your money?

MARK SALLERSON

What happened?

RONNIE NUDELL

Rabbi Turchik took his radio. Had money in it.

MARK SALLERSON

That fucker!

DANNY

Yeah. I think he said he was confiscating it.

MARK SALLERSON

He's a fucker! Where do you get your money?

RONNIE NUDELL

Mike Fagle's gonna kick his ass. Last week he pounded the crap out of Seth Seddlemeyer.

MARK SALLERSON

He's a fucker!

RONNIE NUDELL

Fagle? Or Seth Seddlemeyer?

MARK SALLERSON

They're both fuckers!

BATHROOM DOOR

A hand enters to knock.

UNCLE ARTHUR'S VOICE

Out in a minute!

SARAH

Are you still in there?!

ARTHUR

I, uh . . . Just a minute!

SARAH

I've gotta wash my hair! I'm going out tonight, to The Hole!

23

ARTHUR

Okay! Out in a minute!

OUTSIDE

Larry pulls into the driveway and gets out of his car. The purr of a lawnmower. He looks.

His point-of-view: Mr. Brandt, the next-door neighbor, is mowing his lawn. He has a buzz cut and wears a white T-shirt.

Another noise competes with the lawnmower: rattling, squeaking, gear-grinding. The orange school bus with Hebrew lettering pulls up across the street. Danny emerges.

DINNER TABLE

Larry sits in. His wife and two children are already seated. There is one empty place. Larry projects:

LARRY

Arthur!

A muffled voice:

ARTHUR

Yeah!

LARRY

Dinner!

ARTHUR

Okay! Out in a minute!

LARRY

We should wait.

SARAH

Are you kidding!

They start eating.

LARRY

Mr. Brandt keeps mowing part of our lawn.

JUDITH

Does that matter?

LARRY

What?

JUDITH

Is it important?

Larry shrugs.

LARRY

It's just odd.

JUDITH

Any news on your tenure?

LARRY

I think they'll give me tenure.

JUDITH

You *think*.

LARRY
(*equably*)

Well, I don't *know*. These things aren't, you know . . .

JUDITH

No, I *don't* know. Which is why I ask.

LARRY

Well –

SARAH

Mom, how long is Uncle Arthur staying with us?

JUDITH

Ask your father.

BACK YARD

Twilight.

Larry is stepping onto a hose as he unwheels it from the drum of a travelling sprinkler, laying out an arc to cover the back yard. Intermittent thwacks from next door.

25

Mr. Brandt and his son, who also has a buzz cut and wears a white T-shirt, throw a baseball back and forth. Mr. Brandt throws hard. The ball pops in the boy's mitt.

MITCH

Ow.

Larry walks over to the boundary defined by the fresh mowing. He sights down it.

Mr. Brandt looks over his shoulder at Larry, looking. Mr. Brandt is expressionless. He goes back to throwing.

MITCH

Ow.

INSIDE

Evening. Lights on. Larry sits at the kitchen table, a briefcase open on the chair next to him. Blue books – examination booklets – are spread on the table in front of him. He reads, occasionally making marginal scribbles, grading.

From off, faint and dulled by intervening walls, rock music: somewhere in the house Danny is listening to Jefferson Airplane.

The clink of teaspoon against china as Larry stirs his tea.

Judith enters.

JUDITH

Honey.

LARRY
(*absent*)

Honey.

JUDITH

Did you talk to Sy?

LARRY
(*still absent*)

Sy? – Sy Ableman! – That's right, he called, but I –

JUDITH

You didn't talk to him.

LARRY

No, I –

JUDITH

You know the problems you and I have been having.

Sympathetic, but still absent:

LARRY

Mm.

JUDITH

Well, Sy and I have become very close.

This brings Larry's head up. He focuses on Judith, puzzled. She elaborates:

. . . In short: I think it's time to start talking about a divorce.

Larry stares at her. A long beat.

At length, trying to digest:

LARRY

. . . Sy Ableman!

JUDITH

This is not about Sy.

LARRY

You mentioned Sy!

JUDITH

Don't twist my words. We –

LARRY

A divorce – what have I done! I haven't done anything –
What have I done!

JUDITH

Larry, don't be a child. You haven't "done" anything. I
haven't "done" anything.

LARRY

Yes! Yes! We haven't done anything! And I – I'm probably
about to get tenure!

JUDITH

Nevertheless, there have been problems. As you know.

LARRY

Well –

JUDITH

And things have changed. And then – Sy Ableman. Sy has come into my life. And now –

LARRY

Come into your – what does that mean?! You, you, you, you barely know him!

JUDITH

We've known the Ablemans for fifteen years.

LARRY

Yes, but you – you said we hadn't done anything!

Judith suddenly is stony:

JUDITH

I *haven't* done anything. This is not some flashy fling. This is not about woopsy-doopsy.

Larry stares at her.

LARRY

. . . Sy *Able*man!

From down the hall, a knock on a door. A muffled voice:

ARTHUR

Out in a minute!

JUDITH

Look, I didn't know any other way of breaking it to you. Except to tell you. And treat you like an adult. Is that so wrong?

Larry does not seem to be listening. His eyes roam the room as he thinks.

LARRY

Where do I sleep?

Judith narrows her eyes.

> JUDITH
> *What?*

> LARRY
> Arthur's on the couch!

> JUDITH
> Look. Sy feels that we should –

> LARRY
> Esther is barely cold!

> JUDITH
> Esther died three years ago. And it was a loveless marriage.
> Sy wants a Gett.

This derails the conversation. Larry stares, trying to pick up the thread.

> LARRY
> . . . A what?

> JUDITH
> A ritual divorce. He says it's very important. Without a Gett
> I'm an Aguna.

> LARRY
> A what? What are you talking about?

She turns to go, peeved:

> JUDITH
> You always act so surprised.

As she leaves:

> . . . I have begged you to see the rabbi.

FADE IN

*Larry has fallen asleep at the kitchen table, face down in a pile of blue
books. Cold blue light sweeps across him and he looks up.*

*A short, balding middle-aged man in flannel pyjamas and an old
flannel dressing gown is in front of the open refrigerator holding an*

*open jar of orange juice. He tips the jar back to drink, his free hand
holding a balled-up towel to the back of his neck*

Larry stares at him.

Fade out.

BLEGEN HALL

*Larry enters the departmental office. His eyes are red-rimmed and
dark-bagged. He has beard stubble.*

*The department's secretary wheels her castored chair away from her
typing.*

> SECRETARY
> Messages, Professor Gopnik.

He takes the two phone messages.

HIS OFFICE

Larry looks at the messages:

> WHILE YOU WERE OUT *Dick Dutton of Columbia Record Club*
> CALLED REGARDING: *"2nd attempt. Please call."*

> WHILE YOU WERE OUT *Sy Ableman*
> CALLED REGARDING: *"Let's have a good talk."*

A knock brings his look up.

> LARRY
> Yes – thanks for coming, Clive.

Clive Park enters the office.

> . . . Have a seat.

*Larry uses a key to open the top desk drawer. He takes out the envelope
holding cash.*

> . . . We had, I think, a good talk, the other day, but you left
> something that –

CLIVE

I didn't leave it.

LARRY

Well – you don't even know what I was going to say.

CLIVE

I didn't leave anything. I'm not missing anything. I know where everything is.

Larry looks at him, trying to formulate a thought.

LARRY

Well . . . then, Clive, where did this come from?

He waves the envelope.

. . . This is here, isn't it?

Clive looks at it gravely.

CLIVE

Yes, sir. That is there.

LARRY

This is not nothing, this is something.

CLIVE

Yes, sir. That is something.

A beat.

. . . What is it?

LARRY

You know what it is! You know what it is! I believe. And you know I can't keep it, Clive.

CLIVE

Of course, sir.

LARRY

I'll have to pass it on to Professor Finkle, along with my suspicions about where it came from. Actions have consequences.

CLIVE

Yes. Often.

Always! Actions always have consequences!

He pounds the desk for emphasis.

. . . In this office, actions have consequences!

CLIVE

Yes, sir.

LARRY

Not just physics. Morally.

CLIVE

Yes.

LARRY

And we both know about your actions.

CLIVE

No, sir. *I* know about my actions.

LARRY

I can interpret, Clive. I know what you meant me to
understand.

CLIVE

Meer sir my sir.

Larry cocks his head.

LARRY

. . . "Meer sir my sir"?

CLIVE
(*careful enunciation*)
Mere . . . surmise. Sir.

He gravely shakes his head.

. . . Very uncertain.

CLOSE ON TURNTABLE TONE ARM

A hand lays it onto a slowly spinning vinyl record.

Through scratches and pops, an unaccompanied tenor starts a mournful Hebrew chant.

Close on the sleeve:

RABBI YOUSSELE ROSENBLATT
CHANTS YOUR HAFTORAH PORTION
VOLUME 12

Rabbi Youssele wears a caftan and a felt hat and has sad eyes that peer out, like an owl in foliage, from the dark beard that covers most of the rest of his face.

Wider, on Danny, in his bedroom, evening. He lifts the tone arm on the portable turntable.

He chants the passage.

He drops the tone arm at the same place; Rabbi Youssele chants the passage again.

Danny listens, eyes narrowed. He lifts the tone arm and chants the passage again.

He replays the passage again but before he can lift the tone arm to echo it once more, his door bursts open. Rabbi Youssele continues to chant.

SARAH

You little brat fucker! You snuck twenty bucks out of my drawer!

DANNY

Studying Torah! Asshole!

SARAH

You little brat! I'm telling Dad!

DANNY

Oh yeah? You gonna tell him you've been sneaking it out of his wallet?

SARAH

All right, you know what I'm gonna do? You little brat? If you don't give it back?

We hear the thunk of the front door opening. Danny stands, calling:

DANNY

Dad?

FOYER

Larry is entering with his briefcase. As he stows it in the foyer closet Danny's voice continues, off:

DANNY

Dad, you gotta fix the aerial.

Judith emerges from the kitchen.

JUDITH

Hello, Larry, have you thought about a lawyer?

LARRY

Honey, please!

Danny emerges from the hall.

DANNY

We're not getting Channel 4 at all.

LARRY
(to Judith)

Can we discuss it later?

DANNY

I can't get *F Troop*.

JUDITH

Larry, the children know. Do you think this is some secret?
Do you think this is something we're going to keep quiet?

Sarah enters.

SARAH

Dad, Uncle Arthur is in the bathroom again! And I'm going
to The Hole at eight!

She hits Danny on the back of the head.

DANNY

Stop it!

34

LARRY

Sarah! What's going on!

DANNY

She keeps doing that!

LATER

Larry sits in a reclining chair in the living room, head back, listening to Sidor Belarsky on the hi-fi. From somewhere, a hiss-sucking sound, and the sound of a pencil busily scratching paper.

We cut to the writing: Uncle Arthur sits scribbling into a spiral notebook, his free hand holding the end of a length of surgical tubing against the back of his neck. The tube leads to a Water Pik-like appliance on an end table next to him – the source of the sucking sound.

After listening to the music for a long beat, Larry speaks into space:

LARRY

Arthur?

Uncle Arthur does not look up from his scribbling.

ARTHUR

Yes?

Larry continues to stare at the ceiling.

LARRY

What're you doing?

Still without looking up:

ARTHUR

Working on the Mentaculus.

Long beat. Music. Scribbling.

LARRY

. . . Any luck, um, looking for an apartment?

More scribbling.

ARTHUR

No.

The doorbell chimes.

Larry enters, glances through the front door's head-height window, and – freezes, one hand arrested on its way to the doorknob.

His point-of-view: framed by the window, yellowly lit by the stoop light, a human head. A middle-aged man, a few years older than Larry. A fleshy face with droopy hangdog features, a five-o'clock shadow, and sad Harold Bloom eyes.

Larry opens the door.

> LARRY

Sy.

Sy enters, thrusts out a hand. His voice vibrates with a warm, sad empathy:

> SY

Good to see you, Larry.

He is a heavy-set man wearing a short-sleeved shirt that his belly tents out in front of him. In his left hand he holds a bottle of wine.

> LARRY
> (*tightly*)

I'll get Judith.

> SY

No, actually Larry, I'm here to see you, if I might.

He shakes his head.

. . . Such a thing. Such a thing.

> LARRY

Shall we go in the . . .

He is leading him into the kitchen but Sy, oblivious to surroundings, ploughs on with the conversation, arresting both men in the narrow space between kitchen sink and stove, invading Larry's space.

36

SY

You know, Larry – how we handle ourselves, in this
situation – it's so impawtant.

LARRY

Uh-huh.

SY

Absolutely. Judith told me that she broke the news to you.
She said you were very adult.

LARRY

Did she.

SY

Absolutely. The respect she has for you.

LARRY

Yes?

SY

Absolutely. But the children, Larry. The children.

He shakes his head.

. . . The most impawtant.

LARRY

Well, I guess . . .

SY

Of coss. And Judith says they're handling it so well. A tribute
to you. Do you drink wine? Because this is an incredible
bottle. This is not Mogen David. This is a wine, Larry.
A Bawdeaux.

LARRY

You know, Sy –

SY

Open it – let it breathe. Ten minutes. Letting it breathe, so
impawtant.

LARRY

Thanks, Sy, but I'm not –

SY

I insist! No reason for discumfit. *I'll* be uncumftable if you don't take it. These are signs and tokens, Larry.

LARRY

I'm just – I'm not ungrateful, I'm, I just don't know a lot about wine and, given our respective, you know –

Sy startles him with an unexpected hug.

SY

S'okay.

He finishes the hug off with a couple of thumps on the back.

. . . S'okay. Wuhgonnabe fine.

SKEWED ANGLE ON PARKING LOT

We are dutch on a slit of a view through a cracked-open frosted window: the Hebrew school parking lot.

The last couple of student-filled buses are rolling out of the lot. It is late afternoon.

A reverse shows Danny in a stall, standing on a toilet seat, angling his head to peer out a bathroom window opened at the top.

The bathroom outside the stall: Ronnie Nudell leans against a sink waiting, taking a long draw from a joint.

Danny emerges from the stall. Ronnie Nudell offers the joint:

RONNIE NUDELL

Want some of this fucker?

HALLWAY

The bathroom door cracks open and Danny peeks out.

His point-of-view: the empty hallway ending in a T with another hallway. A janitor crosses the far perpendicular hall, pushing a broom. He disappears. His echoing footsteps recede.

Danny and Ronnie emerge from the bathroom.

RABBI MARSHAK

The photo-portrait on the wall of Mar Turchik's office is lit by late-day sun.

We hear a scraping sound.

Wider: Ronnie Nudell looks over Danny's shoulder as Danny, hunched at Mar Turchik's desk, jiggles the end of a bent hanger in the keyhole of the top-center drawer. The hanger turns.

The boys open the drawer. In it: squirt guns, marbles set to rolling by the opening of the drawer, a comic book, a Playboy *magazine, a slingshot, a small bundle of firecrackers. Hands rifle the gewgaws: no radio.*

RONNIE NUDELL

Fuck.

SANCTUARY

We are behind the two boys, who sit side-by-side in the last pew of the empty sanctuary, gazing off. The stained-glass windows further weaken anemic late-day light. In deference to the location, the boys wear yarmulkas.

A long hold on their still backs.

At length, some movement in Danny's back, his head dips, and we hear him sucking on a joint. He holds it, exhales, and passes it wordlessly to Ronnie Nudell.

SUBURBAN STREET

We pull Danny, eyes red-rimmed, walking along the street, still wearing his yarmulka. It is dusk.

The front door of a house just behind Danny opens. A husky, shaggy-haired youth emerges on the run.

The sound has alerted Danny. Seeing Mike Fagle, he too runs. He reaches up and grabs his yarmulka and clutches it in one of his pumping fists.

Pursued and pursuer both run wordlessly, panting, feet pounding.

Mike Fagle is closing. But Danny is already cutting across the Brandts' front yard, approaching his own. He plunges into the house and slams the door.

Mike Fagle draws up, panting, gazing hungrily at the house.

PUFFY WHITE CLOUDS

A shockingly blue sky hung with picture-perfect clouds.

The top of an aluminum extension ladder swings in from the bottom of the frame and comes toward us.

We cut side-on as the ladder clunks against an eave.

The ladder starts vibrating to the rhythmic clung *of someone climbing.*

Hands enter. Larry's head enters.

He climbs onto the roof.

He takes a couple of hunched steps in from the edge before cautiously straightening, making sure of his balance. He looks around.

His point-of-view toward the front: an unfamiliarly high perspective on the street and the neighboring houses, almost maplike. Very peaceful. Wind gently waves the trees.

Larry gingerly walks up to the aerial at the peak of the roof. He straddles the peak and, reacting to a rhythmic popping noise, looks down toward the back.

Foreshortened Mr. Brandt and Mitch are playing catch in their back yard. With each toss the ball pops, alternately in father's mitt and son's.

MITCH

Ow.

Precariously balanced, Larry reaches up for the aerial. He tentatively touches it. He grasps it. He twists the aerial.

Something strange: as it rotates the aerial creaks – a high whine like the hum sounded from the rim of a wineglass.

MITCH

Ow.

Faintly, under the wineglass sound, and clouded by static, a ringing tenor sings in an unfamiliar modality. Cantorial music.

Larry drops his hand. Inertia keeps the aerial rotating slowly till it dies, the sound drifting away into the sibilant shushing of trees.

Larry reaches out again to turn the aerial. The same crystal hum . . . cantorial singing . . . and now, layering in, the theme from F Troop.

Music. Crystal hum. Wind.

MITCH

Ow.

Larry's look travels: his point-of-view pans slowly off the steep angle on the neighbors' game of catch, travels across his own backyard, and brings in the white fence that encloses the patio of the neighbor on the other side.

MR. BRANDT
(*off*)

Good toss, Mitch.

On the enclosed patio a woman reclines on a lawn chaise of nylon bands woven over an aluminum frame. She is on her back, eyes closed against the sun. She is naked.

MITCH
(*off*)

Ow.

Larry reacts to the naked woman: startled at first, he moves to hide behind the peak of the roof. But as he realises that the sun keeps the woman's eyes closed he relaxes, continuing to stare.

She is attractive. Not young, not old: Larry's age. Peaceful.

After a still beat one of her hands gropes blindly to the side. It finds an ashtray on the table next to her and takes from it a pluming cigarette. She puffs, and replaces it.

(*off*)

Ow.

F Troop. *Cantorial singing.*

Blue sky and white puffy clouds.

The sound of a pencil scratching paper.

NOTEBOOK

A pencil writes equations into a lamplit spiral notebook.

Sidor Belarsky comes in at the cut. So does the spluttering suck-sound of Uncle Arthur's evacuator.

Wider on Uncle Arthur, in his pyjamas, propped up on the narrow fold-out sofa, writing with one hand as he holds the evacuator hose to his neck with the other.

Squeezed into the living room next to the fold-out sofa is a camp cot of plaid-patterned nylon stretched over a folding frame. On the camp cot is Larry, lying half-in, half-out of a rumpled sleeping bag. He stares at the ceiling, a damp washcloth pressed to his forehead. His face is flaming red.

Arthur speaks absently as he scribbles:

ARTHUR
Will you read this? Tell me what you think?

Larry continues to stare at the ceiling.

LARRY
Okay.

Uncle Arthur glances up, focuses on Larry.

ARTHUR
Boy. You should've worn a hat.

LATER

The lights are out. Very quiet. Uncle Arthur lightly snores.

Larry still stares at the ceiling. He shifts his weight. The cot frame squeaks. He shifts again. Another creak.

Larry fishes his watch from the jumble of clothes on the floor: 4:50.

KITCHEN

Larry, in his underwear, spoons ground coffee into the percolator. Uncle Arthur snores on in the other room.

From outside, a dull thunk.

Larry pulls back a curtain.

Next door, Mr. Brandt goes down the walk, wearing camouflage togs and a billed camo cap, a rifle bag slung over his shoulder. He is carrying an ice chest, its contents clicking and sloshing.

The boy Mitch, also wearing camo clothes and cap and also with a rifle bag, has just closed the front door. He now lets the screen door swing shut behind him and follows his father down the walkway to the car in the drive.

The twitter of early morning birds. Mr. Brandt's voice, though not projected, stands out in the pre-dawn quiet:

> MR. BRANDT
> Let's see some hustle, Mitch.

CLOSE ON THE NOTEBOOK

Its top sheet, densely covered by equations, has a heading:

> *The Mentaculus*
> *Compiled by Arthur Gopnik*

After a beat Larry's hand enters to turn the page. The second page is also densely covered with equations.

> VOICE
> Larry?

Larry's look comes up from the Mentaculus. We are in Larry's office. Standing in the office doorway is Arlen Finkle.

43

LARRY

Hi Arlen.

ARLEN FINKLE

Larry, I feel that, as head of the tenure committee, I should tell you this, though it should be no cause for concern. You should not be at all worried.

Larry waits for more. Arlen, though, seems to think it is Larry's turn to speak, and so, after a beat, he does:

LARRY

Okay.

ARLEN FINKLE

I feel I should mention it even though we won't give this any weight at all in considering whether to grant you tenure, so, I repeat – no cause for concern.

LARRY

Okay, Arlen. Give *what* any weight?

ARLEN FINKLE

We have received some letters, uh . . . *denigrating* you, and, well, urging that we not grant you tenure.

LARRY

From who?

ARLEN FINKLE

They're anonymous. And so of course we dismiss them completely.

LARRY

Well . . . well . . . what do they say?

ARLEN FINKLE

They make allegations, not even allegations, *assertions*, but I'm not really . . . While we give them no credence, Larry, I'm not supposed to deal in any specifics about the committee's deliberations.

LARRY

But . . . I think you're saying, these won't play any part in your deliberations.

44

ARLEN FINKLE

None at all.

LARRY

Um, so what are they . . .

ARLEN FINKLE

Moral turpitude. You could say.

LARRY

Uh-huh. Can I ask, are they, are they – idiomatic?

ARLEN FINKLE

I, uh . . .

LARRY

The reason I ask, I have a Korean student, South Korean, disgruntled South Korean, and I meant to talk to you about this, actually, he –

ARLEN FINKLE

No. No, the letters are competently – even eloquently – written. A native English-speaker. No question about that.

LARRY

Uh-huh.

ARLEN FINKLE

But I reiterate this, Larry: no cause for concern. I only speak because I would have felt odd concealing it.

LARRY

Yes, okay, thank you, Arlen.

ARLEN FINKLE

Best to Judith.

Larry answers with a wan smile. He looks down at the Mentaculus.

HEBREW SCHOOL EXTERIOR

Somewhere inside the school a bell rings. Its doors swing open and children emerge.

Our angle is down a line of school buses waiting to ferry the children home, each bus stencilled with the same Hebrew lettering.

We track toward the buses to steepen the rake. As children sort themselves and climb into their respective vehicles, the track brings the nearest bus into the foreground. It noisily idles with its signature squeaks and stress sounds, its low engine rumbling. Children start climbing on.

MINUTES LATER

Inside the bus, now moving. Engine noise bangs in louder and air roars in through open windows. Somewhere on the bus, Jefferson Airplane plays.

We are on the driver, a sallow man in a short-sleeved white shirt with earlocks and a yarmulka. He pitches about, stoically wrestling with the wheel and gear shift as the vehicle bucks.

The pitching children.

> DANNY
> I gotta get my radio back.

> MARK SALLERSON
> Maybe the fucker lodged it up his fucking asshole.

> DANNY
> I gotta get it back. Or Mike Fagle's gonna pound the crap out of me.

> MARK SALLERSON
> Way up his asshole.

> DANNY
> And I'll still have to get my sister the money back or she's gonna break four of my records. Twenty bucks, four records.

> HOWARD ALTAR
> How do you buy all those records? Where do you get your funds?

CLOSE ON LARRY

Standing in his yard. His eyes are darkly pouched. He is staring at something, it seems in dismay. We hear a fluttering sound.

His point-of-view: stakes are set out in the Brandts' yard. Red ribbon connecting them outlines a projection from the side of the house. The loose ends of the ribbon flutter in the breeze.

Engine noise brings Larry's look around. A car is arriving.

It is the Brandts' car, oddly burdened. As it pulls into their driveway we see that there is a four-point stag strapped to the hood, its head lolling over the grille.

Mr. Brandt and Mitch get out of the car in their hunting fatigues. Blood is smeared on Mr. Brandt's shirt.

MR. BRANDT

Go scrub up, Mitch.

LARRY

Uh, good afternoon.

This brings Mr. Brandt's look around. Apparently he is unused to talking with his neighbor. A short beat.

MR. BRANDT

Afternoon.

Behind him is the dead buck, staring off through sightless eyes.

LARRY
(lamely)

. . . Been hunting?

MR. BRANDT

Yep.

LARRY

Is that a, uh . . .

He is indicating the staked area. Mr. Brandt looks at it, looks back at Larry.

MR. BRANDT

Gonna be a den.

LARRY

Uh-huh, that's great. Uh, Mr. Brandt –

47

Mr. Brandt barks at Mitch, who has lingered to listen to the grown-ups:

MR. BRANDT

I said scrub up, Mitch!

The child quickly goes. Larry frowns.

LARRY

Isn't this a school day?

MR. BRANDT

Took him out of school today. So he could hunt with his dad.

LARRY

Oh!

He nods.

. . . That's . . . nice.

Mr. Brandt stares at him with button eyes. Small talk is not his thing.

Larry clears his throat.

. . . Um, Mr. Brandt, that's just about at the property line, there. I don't think we're supposed to get within, what, ten feet –

MR. BRANDT

Property line's the poplar.

LARRY

. . . the . . . ?

MR. BRANDT

Poplar!

LARRY

. . . Well . . . even if it is, you're just about over it –

MR. BRANDT

Measure.

We hear two pairs of pounding footsteps coming up the street.

LARRY

I don't have to measure, you can tell it's –

Line's the poplar.

He indicates.

. . . It's all angles.

Mr. Brandt turns and goes.

Larry turns, reacting to the pounding footsteps. One of the two pairs belongs to Danny, who arrives, slowing to a walk, panting, a bookbag over his shoulder.

A half-block back the pursuing boy also stops running. Husky, shaggy-haired, he watches, scowling, as Danny goes up the walk to his house.

Larry addresses Danny's retreating back:

LARRY

What's going on?

DANNY

Nothing.

IN THE HOUSE

Larry enters.

JUDITH
(off)

Larry?

LARRY
(projecting)

Yeah?

JUDITH
(off)

Did you go to Sieglestein, Schlutz?

LARRY

No, I – not yet.

JUDITH
(off)

Larry.

LARRY

Appointment Monday.

The thud of a car door outside.

Sarah emerges from the hall and heads for the front door, pulling on a jacket. Larry is surprised.

. . . Where are you going?

SARAH

I'm going to The Hole.

LARRY

At five o'clock?

He looks out the front-door window. Four girls have emerged from a car and are coming up the walk. They are Sarah's age and all have dark hair and big noses.

SARAH

We're stopping at Laurie Kipperstein's house so I can wash my hair.

Larry pulls open the door. From the four dark girls:

VOICES

Hi, Mr. Gopnik.

LARRY

You can't wash it here?

From somewhere in the house, Jefferson Airplane starts.

As she brushes past Larry:

SARAH

Uncle Arthur's in the bathroom.

VOICE

Out in a minute!

Judith enters.

JUDITH

Are you ready?

LARRY

Huh?

JUDITH

We're meeting Sy at Embers.

LARRY

I am?

JUDITH

Both of us. I *told* you.

EMBERS

Larry has his arms pinned at his sides by hugging Sy Ableman.

SY

Larry. How are you?

LARRY

Sy.

SY

Hello, Judith.

JUDITH

Hello, Sy.

Sy releases Larry and all seat themselves at Sy's booth – Judith next to Sy, Larry facing.

SY

Thank you for coming, Larry. It's so impawtant that we be able to discuss these things.

LARRY

I'm happy to come to Embers, Sy, but, I'm thinking, really, maybe it's best to leave these discussions to the lawyers.

SY

Of coss! Legal matters, let the lawyers discuss! Don't mix apples and oranges!

JUDITH

I've *begged* you to see the lawyer.

LARRY
(*teeth grit*)
I told you, I'm going Monday.

SY
Monday is timely! This isn't – please! – Embers isn't the forum for legalities, you are so right!

JUDITH
Hmph.

SY
No, Judith and I thought merely we should discuss the practicalities, the living arrangements, a situation that will conduce to the comfit of all the parties. This is an issue where no one is at odds.

Larry isn't sure where this is leading:

LARRY
. . . Living arrangements.

SY
Absolutely. I think we all agree, the children not being contaminated by the tension – the most impawtant.

JUDITH
We shouldn't put the kids in the middle of this, Larry.

LARRY
The kids aren't –

JUDITH
I'm saying "we". I'm not pointing fingers.

SY
No one is playing the "blame game", Larry.

LARRY
I didn't say anyone was!

JUDITH
Well, let's not play "he said, she said", either.

LARRY
I wasn't! I –

52

SY

All right, well let's just step back, and defuse the situation,
Larry.

Larry glares at Sy.

Sy smiles at him, sadly. He reaches over and rests a hand on Larry's.

. . . I find, sometimes, if I count to ten.

A beat.

. . . One . . . two . . . three . . . faw . . . Or silently . . .

Long beat.

JUDITH

Really, to keep things on an even keel, especially now,
leading up to Danny's bar mitzvah –

SY

A child's bar mitzvah, Larry!

JUDITH

Sy and I think it's best if you move out of the house.

LARRY

. . . Move *out*?!

SY

It makes eminent sense.

JUDITH

Things can't continue as they –

LARRY

Move out! Where would I go?!

SY

Well, for instance, the Jolly Roger is quite livable. Not
expensive, and the rooms are eminently habitable.

JUDITH

This would allow you to visit the kids.

SY

There's convenience in its fava. There's a pool –

LARRY

Wouldn't it make more sense for you to move in with Sy?

Judith and Sy gape.

After a beat:

JUDITH

Larry!

SY

Larry, you're jesting!

JUDITH

Larry, there is much to accomplish before that can happen.

Sy sadly shakes his head.

SY

Larry, Larry, Larry. I think, really, the Jolly Roger is the appropriate coss of action.

He shrugs.

. . . It has a pool.

IN BLACK AND WHITE: A BRAIN

It sits in in a large fishbowl, bathed in clear fluid.

The brain pulses, alive. Leads connect it to various pieces of gear outside the fishbowl. Brain and appurtenances are on a dais of sorts, dressed out with bunting.

Oddly, the picture is scored with cantorial singing.

The brain seems to be giving orders to people who wear imperfectly form-fitting 1950s uniforms of the future. After receiving their instructions the minions of the brain bow to it and leave. They are succeeded by two leather-helmeted thugs, big and heavy though lacking muscle definition, who escort a resisting handsome man before the brain. The handsome man, hands tied behind his back, gazes defiantly up at the brain which in some fashion addresses him.

We hear blows and voices over the cantorial music:

DANNY

Stop it!

SARAH

Creep fucker!

DANNY

Stop it! I'm getting it! I'm gonna get it!

Wider shows that the brain is on television, which Danny has muted while he plays the Cantor Youssele Rosenblatt record and drills his Torah portion. He and Sarah are in a stand-off, hands tensed either to deliver or ward off blows.

SARAH

Brat!

Larry enters.

LARRY

What's going on?

SARAH
(*leaving*)

Nothing.

LARRY

What was that?

DANNY

Nothing.

LARRY

How's the haftorah coming? Can you maybe use the hi-fi?

DANNY

What?

We hear the doorbell off. Larry indicates the portable record player.

LARRY

Can I borrow this? I'm taking some stuff. To, you know, the Jolly Roger.

DANNY

Sure, Dad.

On TV the handsome man shouts defiance at the brain.

From off, Sarah projects:

SARAH

Dad. Chinese guy.

ASIAN MAN

A middle-aged Korean man, well groomed, wearing a nicely cut suit and and a jewelled tie pin.

MAN

Culcha clash.

He bangs the knuckles of two fists, illustrating.

. . . Culcha clash.

He faces Larry in the driveway. Larry's car is half-loaded with open boxes that are haphazardly stuffed with clothing and effects.

Larry is leaning against the hood, arms folded, gazing at the man, unimpressed. A beat.

Finally he bestirs himself.

LARRY

With all respect, Mr. Park, I don't think it's that.

MR. PARK

Yes.

LARRY

No. It would be a culture clash if it were the custom in your land to bribe people for grades.

MR. PARK

Yes.

LARRY

So – you're saying it is the custom?

MR. PARK

No. This is defamation. Grounds for lawsuit.

LARRY

You – let me get this straight – you're threatening to sue me for defaming your son?

MR. PARK

Yes.

LARRY

But it would –

MR. BRANDT

Is this man bothering you?

Mr. Brandt is on the strip of lawn separating the two neighbors' driveways. He is giving Mr. Park a hard stare.

LARRY

Is he bothering *me*? No. We're fine. Thank you, Mr. Brandt.

Mr. Brandt, not entirely convinced, withdraws, glaring at the Korean.

Larry turns back to Mr. Park.

. . . I, uh . . . See, if it were defamation there would have to be someone I was defaming him to, or I . . . All right, I . . . let's keep it simple. I could pretend the money never appeared. That's not defaming anyone.

MR. PARK

Yes. And passing grade.

LARRY

Passing grade.

MR. PARK

Yes.

LARRY

Or you'll sue me.

MR. PARK

For taking money.

LARRY

So . . . he did leave the money.

57

MR. PARK

This is defamation.

LARRY

Look. It doesn't make sense. Either he left the money or he
didn't –

MR. PARK

Please. Accept mystery.

LARRY

You can't have it both ways! If –

MR. PARK

Why not?

Larry stares.

We hear Sidor Belarsky music.

RECORD PLAYER

*Sidor Belarsky's singing crosses the cut. The tone arm of Danny's
portable record player rides on a spinning LP.*

*Wider shows Larry grading blue books at a small formica table
crowded into a corner of his motel room. It is a depressingly generic
budget motel room of the mid-sixties with cheaply panelled walls, thin
carpet, formica night tables, plastic lamps and twin beds with stained
nubby bedspreads.*

The phone rings.

LARRY

Hello . . .

He brightens.

. . . Fine, Mimi, how are you? . . . Uh-huh . . . No, it's not
that bad . . .

*Arthur emerges from an alcove in the dim depths of the room that has
a dressing-room mirror and apparently connects to the bathroom. He
has a hand towel pressed to the back of his neck.*

. . . It's not that bad . . . There's a pool . . . Oh sure, that
sounds great . . . Oh, great, then I'll bring Danny . . .

LAKE NOKOMIS

*A crowded beach – children cavorting, adults lounging, much sun, few
umbrellas. Red floats strung with red nylon rope define a swimming
area; beyond it people dive from an anchored raft.*

Splashing and children's laughter slap off the surface of the lake.

WOODS

*Above the lake. The beach noise has some distance and a faintly
bizarre canyon echo. Very present, in contrast, is the rustle of breeze in
trees. It is dark here with intense hot spots where the sun sifts through
the leaf cover.*

*We are close on Danny, who sits leaning back against a tree. After a
very long beat he slowly exhales, a small amount of smoke feathering
out with his breath.*

                              VOICE
        Gimme that fucker.

Danny passes the joint to Ronnie Nudell, who sits opposite.

PICNIC AREA

*Scattered on a woodless rise above the lake are several redwood picnic
tables with, next to each, a firepit.*

*Here in the sun Larry glistens with sweat, as does Mel Nudell, a man
of Larry's age who is bouncing a bag of charcoal briquettes to spill
some into the firepit in the background. Larry sits at the table in the
foreground with Mimi Nudell, who alone seems unaffected by the heat –
or by anything else in the physical environment. Her pale, gravely
composed Giacometti face is shaded by a large-brimmed hat.*

                              LARRY
        No. Almost a year and a half since Touche Ross let him go.
        He's very good with numbers. I think his, his social skills
        have held him back.

MIMI

Such a sweet man though.

LARRY

Arthur has a good heart. And he never complains, unlike me. Sometimes I don't give him enough credit.

MIMI

He tried to tell me about this thing he's working on, this . . .

LARRY

The Mentaculus? He says it's a, uh . . . a probability map. Of the universe. He asked if I could help him publish it. Um, it was a little hard for me to evaluate.

A beat.

MIMI

Does he go out socially at all?

LARRY

He tries. He's been going to the singles mixers at Hillel House. – Well, I should talk, I'm not doing any better.

MIMI

How is Judith?

LARRY

Fine. *She's* fine. I'm the odd man out.

Mimi smiles.

MIMI

Sometimes these things just aren't meant to be. And it can take a while before you feel what was always there, for better or worse.

LARRY

I never felt it! It was a bolt from the blue! What does *that* mean?! Everything that I thought was one way turns out to be another!

MIMI

Then – it's an opportunity to learn how things really are.

Larry broods. Mimi softens.

. . . I'm sorry – I don't mean to sound glib. It's not always easy, deciphering what God is trying to tell you. But it's not something you have to figure out all by yourself. We're Jews, we have that well of tradition to draw on, to help us understand. When we're puzzled we have all the stories that have been handed down from people who had the same problems.

LARRY

I guess.

MIMI

Have you talked to Rabbi Nachtner?

Silence.

Arthur is climbing the hill from the lake, dripping wet. He projects:

ARTHUR

Boy! The air out here is magnificent!

Mimi, looking at Larry, responds to his dark silence:

MIMI

Why not see him?

LARRY

What's the rabbi gonna tell me?

MIMI

If I knew, I'd be the rabbi.

He looks at her glumly. She laughs.

. . . Life is beautiful, Larry. Nobody's sick. Nobody died. You just need help remembering how to enjoy.

Mel Nudell has finished spreading and lighting the coals. He now comes and sits next to Mimi, draping an arm over her shoulder. She strokes his hand.

. . . Where are the kids?

MEL

Woods. Exploring.

Uncle Arthur approaches, swim trunks plastered to his thighs, hair dripping, one hand pressing his towel to the back of his neck.

ARTHUR

If somebody could bottle this air they'd make a million bucks!

A white title:

THE FIRST RABBI

SYNAGOGUE OFFICE ANTEROOM

Larry sits waiting. A door opens and he rises.

LARRY

Oh – Rabbi Scott.

Rabbi Scott Ginzler is the shockingly young junior rabbi.

RABBI SCOTT

Hello, Larry.

LARRY

I thought I was going to see Rabbi Nachtner.

RABBI SCOTT

He was called away on an *etz monim*: Ruth Brynn's mother is in the hospital and she isn't doing well. Rabbi Nachtner asked me to cover for him – come on in.

RABBI SCOTT'S OFFICE

A few minutes later. Larry sits tensely hunched.

LARRY

And she wants a Gett.

A long silence. The hum of ventilation.

At length:

RABBI SCOTT

A what?

LARRY

She wants a –

RABBI SCOTT

Oh, a Gett. Uh-huh, sure.

LARRY

I feel like the carpet's been yanked out from under me.
I don't know which end is up. I'm not even sure how to
react; I'm too confused.

RABBI SCOTT

What reasons did she give? For the rupture?

LARRY

She didn't give – reasons. Just that, oh, you know, things
haven't been going well.

RABBI SCOTT

And is that true?

LARRY

I guess. I don't know. She's usually right about these things.

RABBI SCOTT

Mm-hm.

LARRY

I feel so . . . addled.

RABBI SCOTT

Yes, I can see.

LARRY

I was hoping that . . . Rabbi Nachtner . . .

RABBI SCOTT

That he would . . . yes?

LARRY

Well, with the benefit of his life experience . . . no offense –

Rabbi Scott chuckles.

RABBI SCOTT

No, of course not. I am the junior rabbi. And it's true, the
point of view of somebody who's older and perhaps had

63

similar problems might be more valid. And you should see the senior rabbi as well, by all means. Or even Marshak if you can get in, he's quite busy. But maybe – can I share something with you? Because I too have had the feeling of losing track of *Hashem*, which is the problem here. I too have forgotten how to see Him in the world. And when that happens you think, well, if I can't see Him, He isn't *there* any more, He's gone. But that's not the case. You just need to remember *how* to see Him. Am I right?

He rises and goes to the window.

. . . I mean, the parking lot here. Not much to see.

It is a different angle on the same parking lot we saw from the Hebrew school window.

. . . But if you imagine yourself a visitor, somebody who isn't familiar with these . . . autos and such . . . somebody still with a capacity for wonder . . . Someone with a fresh . . . perspective. That's what it is, Larry.

LARRY

Um . . .

RABBI SCOTT

Because with the right perspective you can see *Hashem*, you know, reaching into the world. He is *in* the world, not just in shul. It sounds to me like you're looking at the world, looking at your wife, through tired eyes. It sounds like she's become a sort of . . . *thing* . . . a problem . . . a thing . . .

LARRY

Well, she's, she's seeing Sy Ableman.

RABBI SCOTT

Oh.

LARRY

She's, they're planning . . . that's why they want the Gett.

RABBI SCOTT

Oh. I'm sorry.

LARRY

It was his idea.

RABBI SCOTT

Well, they do need a Gett to remarry in the faith. But – this is life. For you too. You can't cut yourself off from the mystical or you'll be – you'll remain – completely lost. You have to see these things as expressions of God's will. You don't have to *like* it, of course.

LARRY

The boss isn't always right, but he's always the boss.

RABBI SCOTT

Ha-ha-ha! That's right, things aren't so bad. Look at the parking lot, Larry.

Rabbi Scott gazes out, marvelling.

. . . Just look at that parking lot.

EXTERIOR: GOPNIK HOUSE

Our low angle looks across the lawn toward the front of the house. Pounding footsteps approach and feet enter just off the lens and the person – Danny – quickly recedes, cropping in as he races up to the house.

A beat later pursuing feet enter, slowing, for Danny is already mounting the front stoop. Danny's pursuer does not go deep enough to crop in but we might gather from the size-eleven sneakers and the cuffed jeans that it is hulking Mike Fagle.

GOPNIK KITCHEN

We hear the front door being flung open and slammed shut, and in the background foyer Danny appears, panting heavily. His mother and sister eat soup in the foreground. His sister has a towel wrapped turban-like around her head. One hand keeps the turban in place as she tilts her head down for the soup.

DANNY

We eating already?

SARAH

I'm going to The Hole.

Danny sits at the place set across from his sister. He picks up his spoon.

Some movement in Sarah's body; Danny recoils from a kick.

DANNY

Ow! Cut it out!

JUDITH

What's going on?

The siblings slurp soup, neither answering.

After a couple of slurps:

DANNY

. . . Isn't Dad eating?

JUDITH

He's at the Jolly Roger.

DANNY

Oh yeah.

More slurping.

Fade out.

SIEGLESTEIN, SCHLUTZ

In a small windowless conference room lined by shelves filled with law reference books, Larry rises to greet Don Milgram, entering.

LARRY

Don.

DON

How are you, Larry, Jesus, I am so sorry to be seeing you under these circumstances.

LARRY

Oh, well . . .

DON

I always thought you and Judy were rock solid. This is so terrible, Larry. This is devastating.

LARRY

Well, the way I look at it, it's an opportunity for me to really sit down and figure things out, and, and, look at the world afresh instead of just, you know, settling for the routine, tired old way of looking at things.

Don Milgram stares at him.

DON

. . . Really?

LARRY
(*deflating*)

I don't know. Maybe not.

DON

Well, legally, I have to warn you, it's never easy for the husband. Unless, of course, there's some question of the wife having violated the marriage contract.

LARRY

Oh no, nothing like that. She's planning to marry Sy Ableman, but they –

DON

Sy *Able*man!

LARRY

Yes, but they –

DON

Esther is barely cold!

LARRY

She passed three years ago.

DON

Well, okay, still – this changes the complexion, Larry! Sy *Able*man!

LARRY

Not in the sense that . . . there hasn't been hanky-panky.
To my knowledge.

DON

Oh.

LARRY

No. I'm fairly certain this is not an issue. And in fact they,
uh, Judith wants a Gett.

Beat. Don stares blankly at Larry.

Larry clears his throat.

. . . A ritual divorce.

DON

Oh.

LARRY

So that they can remarry in the faith –

DON

Uh-huh, sure, not really a legal matter. Okay. Well. My
goodness. How are the children taking it?

LARRY

Oh, they're very . . .

He gropes.

. . . resilient.

DON

Good. Well. On the other thing, the neighbor's property
line, I've asked Solomon Schlutz to take a look. There's
very little having to do with real estate that'll get by Sol.

LARRY

Okay. Good. How do you – I guess I'm a little worried,
how do you, I have money pressures and –

DON

Our fee structure? We bill by the hour. Dave Sieglestein and
Solomon Schlutz bill at a hundred and ten, the associates,
me for instance, bill at –

A secretary sticks her head in.

SECRETARY

A call for Mr. Gopnik. Danny. At home.

LARRY

Danny?!

DON

You can take it here.

SECRETARY

Oh-eight-oh-nine.

Larry punches a button on a row of four on the conference-room telephone.

LARRY

Danny?!

VOICE

Dad?

LARRY

Are you all right? Are you all – is everything –

VOICE

F Troop is fuzzy.

LARRY

. . . What?

VOICE

F Troop is still fuzzy.

Larry stares.

DON

Everything okay?

DAWN AT THE JOLLY ROGER

Wide on the motel room, weakly lit by sun starting to seep in around the curtain.

Larry sleeps in one of the twin beds; Uncle Arthur snores in the other.

Uncle Arthur's breath trips and tangles on an impeded inhale and it wakes him, gagging. He blinks, sits up, swings his legs out, gazes blearily around the room.

He rises stiffly and heads for the bathroom.

Larry stirs and looks blearily around.

He stiffly rises. He takes the two steps across the room to the formica desk on which are spread papers for his class. As we hear the sucking sound of the neck evacuator starting up in the bathroom, Larry sweeps papers together and mechanically stuffs his briefcase.

CAR

Larry drives hollow-eyed to work.

After a long beat of staring, the ka-ching *of a bicycle bell.*

Larry's eyes widen and his head swivels, tracking as he overtakes and passes:

The bicyclist. A young Asian man wearing a white traffic mask.

Larry looks at him in the rear-view.

LARRY

Clive!

He frantically pumps down his window, shouting:

. . . Clive! You gonna send your mother next?! You little bastard! I wanna see you! I wanna –

Crash.

He has rear-ended a car stopped at a light.

A blaring horn, a quick second crash of wrenching steel and spattering glass: he has been rear-ended in turn.

The ka-ching *of the bicycle. Clive Park cycles past.*

BLEGEN HALL

Larry enters the outer office, hugging his paper-stuffed briefcase to his chest.

The secretary crooks her phone into her shoulder.

> SECRETARY
>
> Oh – Professor Gopnik. It's Dick Dutton again.

> LARRY
> (*blank*)
>
> Dick Dutton.

LARRY'S OFFICE

He sits in and picks up the phone.

> LARRY
>
> Hello?

> VOICE
>
> Hello, Mr. Gopnik, this is Dick Dutton from the Columbia Record Club. I'm calling because it is now, what, four months and we have yet to receive your first payment.

> LARRY
>
> I – there's some mistake. I'm not a member of the Columbian Record Club.

> VOICE
>
> Sir, you are Laurence Gopnik of 1425 Flag Avenue South?

> LARRY
>
> No, I live at the Jolly Roger.

> VOICE
>
> Excuse me?

> LARRY
>
> No, I – well, yes, okay.

> VOICE
>
> Yes you *are* Laurence Gopnik?

> LARRY
>
> Okay.

> VOICE
>
> Okay means . . .

LARRY

Okay, yes, Laurence Gopnik, yes.

VOICE

Okay, well, you received your twelve introductory albums and you have been receiving the monthly main selection for four months now –

LARRY

"The monthly main selection"? Is that a record? I didn't ask for any records.

VOICE

To receive the monthly main selection you do nothing. You –

LARRY

That's right! I haven't done anything!

VOICE

Yes, that's why you receive the monthly main selection. The last –

LARRY

But I –

VOICE

The last one was Santana Abraxas. You –

LARRY

I didn't ask for Santana Abraxas!

VOICE

You request the main selection at the retail price by doing nothing. It's automatically mailed to you. Plus shipping and handling. You're about to –

LARRY

I can't afford a new record every *month*! I haven't asked for –

VOICE

You're about to get Cosmo's Factory, sir. The June main selection. And you haven't –

LARRY

Look, something is very wrong! I don't want Santana
Abraxas! I've just been in a terrible auto accident!

Beat.

VOICE

I'm sorry, sir.

LARRY

Well – thank you. But I –

VOICE

Are you okay?

LARRY

Yes. Yes, no one was hurt.

VOICE

Okay. Good. Well, you had fourteen days to listen to
Santana Abraxas and return it if you weren't completely
satisfied. You did nothing. And now you –

LARRY

I didn't ask for Santana Abraxas! I didn't listen to Santana
Abraxas! I didn't do anything!

The secretary is sticking her head in.

SECRETARY

Sir . . .

VOICE

Sir. Please. We can't *make* you listen to the record. We –

SECRETARY

Professor Gopnik, your son. He said it's urgent.

LARRY

Okay, look, I have to call you back, this is, this is – I'm
sorry.

He irritably punches a button on the bottom row of four.

. . . Danny?

DANNY

Dad!

LARRY

Did you join the Columbia Record Club?!

Silence.

. . . Danny?

DANNY

Um . . .

LARRY

Danny, this is completely unacceptable. I can't afford to –

DANNY

Okay Dad, but you gotta come home.

LARRY

Is it *F Troop*?

DANNY

Huh? No no. Mom's real upset.

GOPNIK HOUSE

Larry enters. We hear weeping, semi-hysterical, from somewhere in the house.

SARAH'S VOICE

. . . Dad?

LARRY

Yes?

She enters.

SARAH

Does this mean I can't go to The Hole tonight?

LARRY

Does what mean – what happened?

SARAH

Sy Ableman died in a car crash.

74

DANNY'S VOICE

Hey Dad!

LARRY

. . . *What*?!

Danny enters.

DANNY

So are you coming back home? Can you fix the aerial?

The weeping, off, grows louder and more hysterical.

LARRY

What?!

DANNY

It's still, you know . . .

Loud wailing.

Black.

After a beat in black, a white title:

THE SECOND RABBI

RABBI'S OFFICE

We are close on Larry. He sits hunched forward, hands clasped in front of him, staring at the floor, sadly shaking his head.

After a long beat:

LARRY

It seems like she's asking an awful lot. But then – *I* don't know. *Some*body has to pay for Sy's funeral.

Rabbi Nachtner, sitting opposite, nods.

RABBI NACHTNER

Uh-huh.

LARRY

His own estate is in probate. But why does it have to be me? Or is it wrong to complain? Judy says it is. But I'm so strapped for cash right now – paying for the Jolly Roger, and I wrecked the car, and Danny's bar mitzvah . . . I . . .

RABBI NACHTNER

Something like this – there's never a good time.

LARRY

I don't know where it all leaves me. Sy's death. Obviously it's not going to go back like it was.

RABBI NACHTNER

Mm. Would you even want that, Larry?

LARRY

No, I – well yeah! Sometimes! Or – I don't know; I guess the honest answer is I don't know. What *was* my life before? Not what I thought it was. What does it all mean? What is *Hashem* trying to tell me, making me pay for Sy Ableman's funeral?

RABBI NACHTNER

Mm.

LARRY

And – did I tell you I had a car accident the same time Sy had his? The same instant, for all I know. Is *Hashem* telling me that Sy Ableman is me, or we are all one, or something?

RABBI NACHTNER

How does God speak to us: it's a good question. You know Lee Sussman?

LARRY

Dr. Sussman? I think I – yeah?

RABBI NACHTNER

Did he ever tell you about the goy's teeth?

LARRY

No . . . I – What goy?

RABBI NACHTNER

So Lee is at work one day; you know he has the orthodontic practice there at Texa-Tonka.

LARRY

Uh-huh.

RABBI NACHTNER

Right next to the Gold Eagle Cleaners.

We cut to sign for "The Gold Eagle Cleaners". It dominates a small suburban strip mall.

Rabbi Nachtner continues in voice-over as we cut to a frosted glass door with a painted-on "Leon Sussman, DDS".

RABBI NACHTNER

He's making a plaster mold – it's for corrective bridge work – in the mouth of one of his patients . . .

A close shot of a man's mouth biting down on two horseshoe-shaped troughs – an upper and a lower – that overflow goo.

. . . Russell Kraus. He's a delivery dispatcher for the *Star and Tribune* with chronic mandibular deterioration.

The grinding guitar solo from Jefferson Airplane's "Bear Melt" scores the narrative.

The patient opens his mouth as a hand enters to grab the upper tray.

The reverse shows Dr. Sussman, a middle-aged man dressed in the high-collared white smock of an oral surgeon. He takes the mold to a drying table.

Kraus twists over the side of the chair and spits into the water-swirled spit-sink.

. . . Well, the mold dries and Lee is examining it one day before fabricating an appliance . . .

Another day: Dr. Sussman sits at his workbench examining the lower mold. He notices something unusual.

. . . He notices something unusual.

Sussman reaches up for the loupe attached to his eyeglasses.

There seems to be something engraved on the inside of the patient's lower incisors . . .

77

He flips down the loupe. One eye is hugely magnified as he stares.

> . . . Sure enough, it's writing.

Sussman squints.

His point-of-view: tiny incised Hebrew letters.

הושיטגי

Back to Rabbi Nachtner: he confirms with a nod.

> RABBI NACHTNER
> This in a goy's mouth, Larry.

Back to Leon Sussman: the rabbi's narrative continues.

> RABBI NACHTNER
> *Hey vav shin yud ayin nun yud.* "*Hoshiyani.*" "Help me."
> "Save me."

Sussman flips the loupe away and looks off, haunted. He rises.

> . . . He checks the mold, just to be sure. Oh, it's there all
> right . . .

*A dental mirror is dipped into the horseshoe-shaped hardened paste of
the mold. It pans tiny letters that stand out in relief, right side around
in the mirror:*

הושיטגי

Sussman leans back, thinking.

> He calls the goy back on the pretense of needing additional
> measurements for the appliance.

*Close on Kraus grinning as he shakes Sussman's hand in the reception
area. Sussman gestures to invite Kraus back to the examining room.*

> Sussman chats, affecting nonchalance.

*In the examining room, leaning over Kraus in the chair, the dentist is
indeed chatting with apparent casualness.*

> Notice any other problems with your teeth? Anything
> peculiar, et cetera?

Sussman unpockets a dental mirror.

No. No. No. Visited any other dentist recently? No.

He dips the mirror into Kraus's mouth:

הושיטגי

Sussman frowns.

There it is. "Help me"?

He leans back.

Sussman goes home. Can Sussman eat? Sussman can't eat.

Sussman sits at the kitchen table, untouched food in front of him. His wife chats volubly while Sussman stares into space.

Can Sussman sleep? Sussman can't sleep.

Sussman is in bed, pyjamas buttoned to the neck, staring at the ceiling.

What does it mean? Is it a message for him, for Sussman? And if so, from whom? Does Sussman know? Sussman doesn't know.

At a row of shelves, back in the dental office, Sussman pulls down boxes containing other molds.

Sussman looks at the molds of his other patients, goy and Jew alike, seeking other messages. He finds none. He looks in his own mouth . . .

Sussman in pyjamas, in front of a medicine-cabinet mirror, holds in his own mouth a dental mirror and strains to see the reflection of the reflection.

. . . Nothing. His wife's mouth . . .

Sussman's wife lies asleep on her back, her mouth open, snoring softly. Sussman, in pyjamas but with his glasses on and loupe in place, lies over her in bed, supporting himself with one arm thrown across her body. He leans awkwardly in, taking care not to disturb his wife as he lowers a dental mirror into her open mouth.

. . . Nothing. It is a singular event. A mystery.

The Jefferson Airplane guitar solo is heating up.

> But Sussman is an educated man. Not the world's greatest sage, maybe, no Rabbi Marshak, but he knows a thing or two from the Zohar and the Cabalah. He knows every Hebrew letter has its numeric equivalent.

Sussman, still in his pyjamas, is sitting at the kitchen table scribbling on a tablet of lined paper.

Close on the paper: the Hebrew letters have been transcribed into their numeric equivalents:

הושיטגי

374-4548

Nachtner continues in voice-over:

> Seven digits – a phone number maybe?

Sussman reaches for the phone. He hesitates, then dials.

> . . . Sussman dials. It rings.

An elevated cubicle in a grocery store. A man in a white short-sleeved shirt reaches for the phone.

RABBI NACHTNER

> It's a Red Owl grocery store in Bloomington. Hello? Do you know a goy named Kraus? Russell Kraus?

The store manager shakes his head.

> Where have I called? The Red Owl. In Bloomington. Thanks so much.

The manager, puzzled, hangs up.

> Sussman thinks, "Am I supposed to go to the Red Owl, to receive a further sign?" He goes . . .

In the parking lot of the Red Owl, Sussman, wearing a short-brimmed fedora, emerges from his car. It is an unremarkable grocery store in a suburban mall.

> It's a Red Owl.

Inside, Sussman, in his fedora, gazes around.

Groceries. What have you.

A service alley behind the store: dumpsters, wind-blown garbage, Sussman looking.

On the wall behind the store, a stain . . .

There is an old, rather nondescript stain of some liquid splatted against the back wall and long since dried.

. . . Could be a *nun sofit* . . . Or maybe not . . .

The parking lot again: Sussman gets back in his car.

Sussman goes home. What does it mean? He has to find out, if he's ever to sleep again.

Sussman, again in pyjamas buttoned to the neck, lies in bed staring at the ceiling.

He goes to see the rabbi, Nachtner. He comes in and sits right where you're sitting now.

Sussman is indeed sitting across from Rabbi Nachtner, just where we've seen Larry sitting.

What does it mean, Rabbi? Is it a sign from *Hashem*? "Help me." I, Sussman, should be doing something to help this goy? Doing what? The teeth don't say. I should know without asking? Or maybe I'm supposed to help people generally – lead a more righteous life? Is the answer in Cabalah? In Torah? Or is there even a question? Tell me, Rabbi – what can such a sign mean?

Nachtner – not the narrating Nachtner but the Nachtner in the scene – nods and considers.

The rabbi's office in present: Larry stares at the rabbi. He waits a good beat.

He prompts:

LARRY
So what did you tell him?

The rabbi seems surprised by the question.

RABBI NACHTNER

Sussman?

LARRY

Yes!

RABBI NACHTNER

Is it . . . relevant?

LARRY

Well – isn't that why you're telling me?

RABBI NACHTNER

Mm. Okay. Nachtner says, look . . .

The consultation scene again, with the rabbi once again narrating in voice-over. He silently advises the fretful Sussman in sync with his recounting of the same.

. . . The teeth, we don't know. A sign from *Hashem*, don't know. Helping others, couldn't hurt.

Back to the rabbi's office in present. Larry struggles to make sense of the story.

LARRY

But – was it for him, for Sussman? Or –

RABBI NACHTNER

We can't know everything.

LARRY

It sounds like you don't know *anything*! Why even tell me the story?

RABBI NACHTNER
(*amused*)
First I should tell you, then I shouldn't.

Larry, exasperated, changes tack:

LARRY

What happened to Sussman?

Sussman, back in his office, works on different patients as the rabbi resumes the narrative in voice-over.

RABBI NACHTNER

What *would* happen? Not much. He went back to work. For a while he checked every patient's teeth for new messages; didn't see any; in time, he found he'd stopped checking. He returned to life.

Sussman, at home, chats with his wife over dinner.

. . . These questions that are bothering you, Larry – maybe they're like a toothache. We feel them for a while, then they go away.

Sussman lies in bed sleeping, smiling, an arm thrown across his wife.

Back in the rabbi's office, Larry is dissatisfied.

LARRY

I don't want it to just go away! I want an answer!

RABBI NACHTNER

The answer! Sure! We all want the answer! But *Hashem* doesn't owe us the answer, Larry. *Hashem* doesn't owe us anything. The obligation runs the other way.

LARRY

Why does he make us feel the questions if he's not going to give us any answers?

Rabbi Nachtner smiles at Larry.

RABBI NACHTNER

He hasn't told me.

Larry rubs his face, frustrated.

A last question occurs to him:

LARRY

And what happened to the goy?

Rabbi Nachtner's forbearing smile fades into puzzlement.

RABBI NACHTNER

The goy? Who cares?

EXTERIOR: THE SYNAGOGUE

The modern synagogue grafted onto a patch of prairie.

An echoing voice rings out:

VOICE
Sy Ableman was a serious man!

RABBI NACHTNER

In close-up he gazes around, weighing the effect of the words just delivered.

After a beat during which he seeks to establish eye contact with as much of his audience as possible:

RABBI NACHTNER
Sy Ableman was a man devoted to his community . . .

Wider shows Rabbi Nachtner and the congregation facing each other across a casket that rests below the bema.

. . . to Torah study . . .

Larry sits among the congregants, his gaze fixed on a point off.

. . . to his beloved wife Esther until, three years ago, she
passed . . .

Larry's point-of-view: Judith is visible from three-quarters behind. She sits a few rows forward looking weepily up at the rabbi.

. . . and to his duty, as he saw it. Where does such a man
go? A *tzadik* – who knows, maybe even a *lamid vovnik* – a
man beloved by all, a man who despised the frivolous?
Could such a *serious* man . . . simply . . . disappear?

The words echo.

Again the rabbi gazes around, as if awaiting answer.

Then:

. . . We speak of *olam ha-ba*, the World to Come. Not
heaven. Not what the gentiles think of as afterlife. "*Olam*

ha-ba." What is *olam ha-ba*? *Where* is *olam ha-ba*? Well: it is not a *geographic* place, certainly. Like – Canada.

Murmured chuckles from the congregation.

Nor is it the *eretz zavat chalav ood'vash* – the land flowing with milk and honey, for we are not promised a *personal* reward, a gold star, a first-class VIP lounge where we get milk and cookies to eternity!

More chuckles.

Olam ha-ba . . . is in the bosom of Abraham. *Olam ha-ba* is in the soul of this community which nurtured Sy Ableman and to which Sy Ableman now returns. That's right, he returns. Because he still inspires us, *Sy Ableman returns.* Because his memory instructs us, *Sy Ableman returns.* Because his thoughts illuminate our days and ways, *Sy Ableman returns.* The frivolous man may vanish without a ripple but Sy Ableman? Sy Ableman *was a serious man* . . .

A sob echoes through the sanctuary.

Larry looks at Judith, who stifles further sobs with a handkerchief.

. . . As you know, the mourner's kaddish does not mention the dead. It praises *Hashem*; it praises what abides. And Sy Ableman, whose spirit will continue to assist us in *tikkun olam,* is with us even now, a serious man who would say as we now say, *Yiskadal v'yiskadash sh'may rabah* . . .

The congregation rises and chants along until it and Judith's weeping are cut off by:

A HAND RAPPING AT A DOOR

The front door of the Gopnik home.

Larry, still in his suit and yarmulka from shul, opens the door. He recoils in surprise edged with fear.

Reverse: two uniformed policemen.

COP I

Arthur Gopnik?

85

Larry is momentarily dumb. Behind him, in the living room, we see a corner of a card table upon which food has been laid out. Sarah sits with her back to us, head wrapped in a towel-turban. Arthur, on the far side of the table, his balding head yarmulka-topped, half-leans out so that he may sneak looks toward the men at the door while still somewhat hidden. From somewhere down the hall come Judith's muffled sobs.

. . . Are you Arthur Gopnik?

COP 1

LARRY

I'm . . . Laurence Gopnik.

COP 1

Do you go by the name Arthur Gopnik?

LARRY

No.

COP 1

Is that Arthur Gopnik?

Arthur ducks away.

From inside the living room:

DANNY
(off)

Dad? What's going on?

LARRY

Can you tell me what's going on? We're sitting *shiva* here.

COP 1

You're *what*?

LARRY

A religious observance. We're . . . bereaved.

The heretofore wordless second cop gazes in over his partner's shoulder.

COP 2

Who died?

LARRY

My wife's, um . . . it's a long story.

86

Look. Tell Gopnik – Arthur Gopnik – he's breaking the law. We're not arresting him now but next time we will. Gambling is against the law in this state. That's just the way it is. All right. Go back to your . . .

COP 2

Sorry, sir.

LIVING ROOM

A minute later. The family – except for Judith, whose weeping continues off – sits around the card table. A long beat.

At length:

DANNY

Dad, we get Channel 4 now but not Channel 7.

LARRY

Arthur, how could you do that to this family? On Sy's . . . on Sy's –

ARTHUR

It's a victimless crime.

LARRY

That doesn't make it right! And you –

DANNY

He won a lot of money, Dad! The Mentaculus really works!

Larry's gaze swings to his son.

LARRY

You knew about it?!

DANNY

Well, um . . .

ARTHUR

They must have finked me out. They knew I could just keep on winning, so a couple weeks ago they blackballed me, and now they've –

LARRY

What did you do with the money you won?

Silence. Arthur sneaks a look at Danny.

Larry looks back and forth between them.

. . . What's going on?

Arthur shrugs.

ARTHUR

I didn't want it. Danny said he could use it –

SARAH

Unfair!

LARRY

What have you been –

ARTHUR

What's unfair is these guys saying I can't play in their card game!

SARAH

Why give *him* the money?! You know what he spends it on?

LARRY
(*knowing nod*)
I know about the records.

SARAH

Records?! You think he buys *records* from Mike Fagle?

Movement in Danny's body; Sarah recoils from a kick.

. . . Ow! Little brat!

LARRY

Hey! What's going on!

DANNY

At least I'm not saving up for a nose job!

LARRY

What?!

SARAH

Brat!

LARRY

Nobody in this house is getting a nose job! You got that?!

DANNY

Ah!

Struck by a thought he leaps up and bolts from the room.

LARRY

Danny! You weren't excused! We're still talking!

SARAH

What a brat.

LARRY

What was this card game, Arthur?

ARTHUR

Some goys run a private game.

We hear the TV going on in a bedroom and the theme from F Troop.

. . . I think they're Italians.

LARRY

Danny, what's going on!

He rises.

BEDROOM

Larry enters to look down at Danny's back. Beyond him F Troop *flickers on the TV.*

LARRY

Danny! We're sitting *shiva*!

DON MILGRAM'S OFFICE

Larry has his head down on his arms on Don's desktop.

DON

She's retained Barney Silver at Tuchman, Marsh. This is a,
uh – this is an aggressive firm, Larry.

LARRY
(*muffled*)

Uh-huh.

DON

These are not pleasant people. Judith is free of course to
retain whoever she . . . I take it you don't talk to her?

Larry raises his head, squinting.

LARRY

It's hard. I think she emptied our bank account. I tried to
ask her about it, very civilly.

DON

Mm.

LARRY

She, uh . . .

DON

Yeah, yeah, you better open an account in your name only,
put your paychecks in there from here on out. Till we know
where we stand.

LARRY

Can I?

DON

Oh, absolutely!

LARRY

That's not, um, dishonest?

DON

Oh, absolutely! You, uh –

LARRY

I hate to say this, but I think she's also been sneaking cash
out of my wallet.

Oh boy. Well, yes, this is definitely, um, adversarial. The first thing we – are you all right?

Larry is shaking. His eyes are squeezed shut. His mouth is twisting into strange shapes.

. . . Larry!

Now weeping sounds come out, despite Larry's efforts to choke them off.

. . . Larry! It's okay! There's no need for that!

Larry nods, trying to stopper his sobs, waving a hand in the air, signalling that he is all right and will speak when able.

. . . Larry, we can get through this thing!

THE OFFICE

Minutes later.

Larry sits panting but composed, a glass of water in front of him.

After a long beat:

DON

Have you seen the rabbi?

Through his deep breaths:

LARRY

I talked to Nachtner.

DON

Was he helpful at all?

Larry gives a helpless shrug.

Don rolls his eyes.

DON

What – did he tell you about the goy's teeth? You should talk to Marshak.

They told me . . . Marshak . . . doesn't do . . . pastoral work
any more. He just – congratulates the bar mitzvah boy
every week.

DON

That's too bad. A very wise man, Marshak.

Larry sadly shakes his head.

LARRY

Getting old.

DON

Very old.

LARRY

No, me.

DON

Larry, you're fine. It's a bump in the road.

BLEGEN HALL

*Larry walks into the outer office clutching his briefcase. The secretary
is at her typewriter but holding the phone, one hand covering its
mouthpiece.*

SECRETARY

Dick Dutton. Columbia Record Club.

LARRY

Not now.

LARRY'S OFFICE

Larry has the phone to his ear. He listens for a beat.

LARRY

Does he ever come to the phone? If I came in – How about
at Rabbi Marshak's convenience? Uh-huh . . . Uh-huh . . .
Well, could I give you my number at the Jolly Roger?

CLASSROOM

We are close over Larry's shoulder as he scribbles symbols onto the chalkboard.

LARRY
 . . . and *that* means . . . so that . . . from which we derive . . .

His glances back toward the class show him to be wearier, baggier-eyed, more haggard than ever. And there is something odd about his posture.

He makes his writing smaller and smaller so as to finish before hitting the right edge of the chalkboard.

 . . . and also . . . which lets us . . . and . . .

Wider as he finishes and straightens up, revealing that he has been stooping to write across the very bottom of the board.

The equation covers every inch of the classroom-wide three-panelled chalkboard. Larry is an off-balance figure at the right edge of frame.

Reverse on the class: staring.

 . . . Okay?

Larry claps chalk dust from his hands.

 . . . The Uncertainty Principle. It proves we can't ever really know . . . what's going on.

A bell sounds. The students shake off their stupor and rise. Larry projects over the wallah:

 . . . But even if you can't figure anything out, you'll still be responsible for it on the mid-term.

The students disperse to reveal one person still seated:

Sy Ableman.

He wears a prayer shawl and yarmulka.

Larry does not seem surprised to see him.

 . . . Did you follow that?

SY

Of coss. Except that I know what's going on. How do you explain?

LARRY

Well, it might be that, in, you know, in *olam ha-ba* –

SY

Excuse me. Not the issue. In *this* world, Larry.

He nods at the chalkboard.

. . . I'll concede that it's subtle. It's clevva. But at the end of the day, is it convincing?

LARRY

Well – yes it's convincing. It's a proof. It's mathematics.

SY

Excuse me, Larry. Mathematics. Is the art of the possible.

Larry's brow furrows.

LARRY

I don't think so. The art of the possible, that's . . . I can't remember . . . something else . . .

SY

I'm a serious man, Larry.

LARRY

I know that. So if I've got it wrong, what do I –

Sy Ableman holds up one hand to silence him.

SY

So simple, Larry. See Marshak.

LARRY

I *know*, I *want* to see Marshak! I *want* to see Marshak! They told me that – *ooph!*

Without our having seen him rise or cross the room, Sy Ableman has arrived to body-slam Larry into the chalkboard. Now he grabs Larry by the hair and whips his head against the equation. He slams Larry's head again and again, making the chalkboard chatter and the fringes on his own tallis dance.

See Marshak! See Marshak! I fucked your wife, Larry! I
seriously fucked her! *That's* what's going on! See Marshak!

LARRY

*Close on his eyes opening. His head is on a pillow. Dull early light.
A hissing sound.*

Larry looks blearily into the depth of the motel room.

*On the vanity table just outside the bathroom door sits Uncle Arthur's
cyst evacuator, humming and hissing. Its waggling hose snakes through
the cracked-open door.*

MEZUZA

On a doorpost.

*A hand enters to knock. A long beat. The person knocking gives up
and his footsteps start to go away just as the door opens to reveal an
attractive woman – the sunbathing neighbor, now wearing plaid shorts
and a white blouse.*

*Reverse: Larry, frozen halfway down the stoop, head turned back up
toward the door.*

WOMAN
Mr. Gopnik.

LARRY
Oh. Hello, Mrs Samsky. I knocked, and then thought you
weren't here. I, uh . . .

Mrs. Samsky's voice is soft and breathy:

MRS. SAMSKY
It just took me a second to get to the door. I was out back.

Larry stands nodding.

He seems to need a prompt. Mrs. Samsky supplies one:

. . . Can I help you? Wanna come in?

LARRY

No, I –

She steps back.

MRS. SAMSKY

It's cooler.

LARRY

Oh. Okay. I just wanted to let you know . . .

INSIDE

The dimness inside the home Larry enters does indeed suggest coolness. Larry looks around the living room. Wavering light sifts through closed vertical blinds which drift and click over floor-vented air conditioning.

Mrs. Samsky closes the door behind him, shutting out all sound from the street.

LARRY

I've noticed that Mr. Samsky isn't around, and I –

MRS. SAMSKY

He travels.

LARRY

Uh-huh. Yeah, I never seem to see him, so I thought I should let you know, since you're somewhat new here, if you ever have, whatever, chores that you'd, um, or just help with something – I've decided to help others – you know, in a neighborly way . . .

She gazes at him, waiting for the speech to dribble away to silence. In the ensuing beat, quiet except for the clicking of the blinds, she is perfectly still. Finally, only her mouth moves:

MRS. SAMSKY

How thoughtful.

Larry shrugs off the compliment:

LARRY

Oh it's nothing. It's just good to know your neighbors. And

to help. Help others. Although I don't care much for my neighbors on the other side, I must say.

Mrs. Samsky lets more time elapse before responding.

> MRS. SAMSKY
> Goys, aren't they?

> LARRY
> Mm. Very much so. Maybe it's not fair to judge; I have to admit I –

> MRS. SAMSKY
> Won't you sit down?

> LARRY
> Oh! Um. Okay. Thank you.

> MRS. SAMSKY
> Iced tea? I have some.

She is already turning to the kitchen.

> LARRY
> Okay.

He watches her and reacts to:

The backs of her thighs. The flesh retains the broad cross-hatch of her lawn chair.

She disappears into the kitchen, but projects:

> MRS. SAMSKY
> I don't see you around much, either.

> LARRY
> Yes. Actually I haven't been home a lot recently, I, uh, my wife and I are, uh, well, she's got me staying at the Jolly Roger, the little motel there on –

Mrs. Samsky is re-entering with iced tea in two tall glasses beaded with moisture. The click of the ice cubes joins the clicking of the blinds.

> MRS. SAMSKY
> You're in the doghouse, huh?

97

She hands him a glass and sits on the couch next to him, not invasively close, one bare leg folded beneath her.

> LARRY
>
> Yeah, that's an understatement I guess, I – thank you –
> I, uh –

> MRS. SAMSKY
>
> Do you take advantage of the new freedoms?

Larry stares at her. Mrs. Samsky gazes back. Her look displays equanimity; his, not.

Finally:

> LARRY
>
> . . . What do you mean?

Her look holds for one more beat and then she swivels and opens the drawer of an end table.

She turns back with a joint.

> MRS. SAMSKY
>
> It's something I do. For recreation.

She lights it.

> LARRY
>
> That's . . . marijuana?

> MRS. SAMSKY
>
> Mm-hmm.

She hands the joint over.

> . . . You'll find you'll need the iced tea.

Larry handles the bitty cigarette with trepidation.

> LARRY
>
> Is it . . . well . . . okay . . .

THE VERTICAL BLINDS

Some minutes later. They drift and click in the air blown from the floor vents.

Larry stares at them.

After a long beat:

>LARRY

Maybe Rabbi Scott was right.

>MRS. SAMSKY

Who's Rabbi Scott?

>LARRY

The junior rabbi.

>MRS. SAMSKY

The junior rabbi.

Another long beat. Neither person feels compelled to speak.

The joint makes another trip back and forth.

Then:

>. . . What did he say?

>LARRY

He spoke of . . . perception. All my problems are just . . .
just a . . . a mere . . .

He trails off, listening.

>. . . Is that a siren?

>MRS. SAMSKY

No. Some people get a little paranoid when they . . . Holy
cow . . . That *is* a siren.

OUTSIDE

The Samskys' door bursts open and Larry stumbles out. He stares.

*The police car has stopped in front of his own house next door, lightbar
still flashing. Two cops are going up the walk, escorting Uncle Arthur
in handcuffs.*

Larry, stunned, walks woodenly toward his house.

>LARRY

Hey!

Neither the cops nor Uncle Arthur has heard. They have rung the doorbell and now disappear inside.

Larry calls louder –

> . . . HEY!

– and starts to sprint. Behind him Mrs. Samsky has emerged from her house.

At his house Larry takes the stoop steps two at a time. His door stands open and the theme from F Troop *issues from within.*

Just inside the two policemen stand with their backs to us and Uncle Arthur in between. The three men face Danny, who addresses them, projecting over the music from the TV.

> DANNY
>
> Sort of. He sleeps on the couch.

> LARRY
>
> This is crazy!

This brings the cops' look around. Uncle Arthur also turns, shamefaced, to Larry.

> COP
>
> Does this man live here?

> ARTHUR
>
> I didn't know what to tell them! They asked for my address –

> LARRY
>
> It's just mathematics! You can't arrest a man for mathematics!

> ARTHUR
>
> I didn't know whether to say I lived here or at the Jolly Roger.

> COP
>
> You know this man?

> ARTHUR
>
> I figured this would sound more . . . I don't know . . .

Mrs. Samsky appears behind Larry on the stoop.

> DANNY
> Dad, why is Uncle Arthur in handcuffs?

> LARRY
> It's all a mistake. I mean, not a mistake, a, a –

> ARTHUR
> Hello, Mrs Samsky.

> LARRY
> – a *mis*carriage –

> COP
> Does this man live here?

> DANNY
> He sleeps on the couch.

> LARRY
> Look! What did he do!

> ARTHUR
> Nothing! I didn't do anything!

> DANNY
> It folds out. Dad sleeps on a cot.

> LARRY
> You can't just –

> COP
> Sir, we picked this man up at the North Dakota.

Larry is brought up short.

> LARRY
> . . . The North Dakota!

> ARTHUR
> But I didn't *do* anything!

> DANNY
> Dad, what's the North Dakota?

COP

Solicitation. Sodomy. Very serious.

LARRY

. . . The North Dakota!

DANNY

What's sodomy, Dad?

LAW OFFICE CONFERENCE ROOM

Don Milgram sits thinking, bouncing steepled fingers against his nose. Larry waits for his analysis.

Finally:

DON

What does Arthur say?

LARRY

He says he didn't do anything.

DON

Uh-huh.

LARRY

He says . . . he just went in for a drink.

DON

Uh-huh.

Long beat.

. . . Does Arthur drink?

LARRY

No.

DON

Uh-huh.

LARRY

. . . He says he was confused.

DON

Uh-huh. Uh-huh. Well. The North Dakota. Well. You'll need a criminal attorney.

                    LARRY

Okay. Who's –

                    DON

Ron Meshbesher.

                    LARRY

Is he good?

                    DON

Ron is very good.

Larry's gaze wanders. He becomes wistful.

                    LARRY

I don't understand. He goes to mixers at the Hillel House.

                    DON

Mm.

A beat.

. . . I would call Ron Meshbesher.

                    LARRY

Is he expensive?

                    DON

Ron is not cheap.

An uncomfortable beat, broken by a knock at the door. Don projects:

Yeah?

The door cracks open. A pipe edges in, followed by a peeking face: Solomon Schlutz.

. . . Oh, good! Sol, come on in, we could use some good news.

Solomon Schlutz is a large man in shirtsleeves and suspenders. He has the smooth impassive face of a sphinx with a pipe clenched in its teeth.

He glides into the room, a sheaf of files tucked under one arm.

. . . Sol has been looking into the property-line issues . . .

Solomon Schlutz seats himself at the conference table and starts sorting and arranging the files into three piles.

> . . . He wouldn't tell me the details but he seems to think there's a nifty way out of this. Says it was pure luck that he caught something.

A confirming grunt from Solomon Schlutz as he continues to arrange the files, his eye occasionally lingering on a specific page.

> . . . I guess that's why you're full partner, huh Sol?

This sally does not even earn a grunt from Solomon Schlutz, who continues to shuffle papers into order, now and then pausing to squint.

Don smiles at Larry and fills the silence:

> . . . Danny's bar mitzvah is . . . ?

LARRY

This week.

DON

This shabbas! Great!

Solomon Schlutz clears his throat and both men instantly give him their attention.

He carefully justifies the edges of the closest pile of papers, takes the pipe from his mouth, gives Larry a smile that seems to take some effort, and then taps the pipe in a large glass ashtray.

He looks up again at Larry, this time shocked. His stunned look on Larry holds for a long beat.

Larry returns a bewildered look.

Solomon Schlutz, staring at Larry as if he were some sort of monster, emits one barking syllable:

SOLOMON SCHLUTZ

Gah!

His stare holds. He reddens.

DON

. . . Sol?

Solomon Schlutz's face travels from the red end of the spectrum to the violet.

> SOLOMON SCHLUTZ
> Nnnnff!

The pipe clatters out of his hand. The hand grabs at his own shirt front.

> . . . Glufffl . . .

Now his head pitches back. His backflung weight and twisting body send his chair tipping over, one hand still clutching at his chest while the other frantically waves. He disappears behind the conference table and lands with a floor-shaking thump. His writhing and gurgling remain audible.

> DON
> Sol! Sol!

Don Milgram has risen to look down at his fallen colleague; now he flings open the conference room door and bellows into the office:

> An ambulance! Quick! Somebody call an ambulance! A doctor!

A secretary looks in and screams.

> SOLOMON SCHLUTZ
> Garf! . . . Nnlogl . . .

BLEGEN HALL

Larry walks into the outer office clutching his briefcase, eyes wide, shell-shocked. The secretary looks up from her phone.

> SECRETARY
> Dick Dutton. Columbia Record Club.

> LARRY
> Heart attack. Call back.

HIS OFFICE

Larry sits in heavily behind his desk.

A beat.

He opens the top-left desk drawer. He withdraws the bulging white envelope and opens its flap.

He runs a finger over the wad of bills.

VOICE

Larry?

He looks up, startled.

Arlen Finkle stands in the doorway.

. . . As you know, the tenure committee meets – are you all right?

Larry sits frozen, holding the envelope.

LARRY

I'm . . . fine.

ARLEN FINKLE

I'm sorry. I know you've hit a rough patch.

LARRY

Thank you. I'm fine.

He puts the envelope in the desk drawer and closes it.

ARLEN FINKLE

Uh-huh. Well. As you know, the tenure committee meets next Wednesday to make its final determinations. If there's –

LARRY

Arlen, I am not an evil man!

Arlen looks at him, shocked.

ARLEN FINKLE

Larry! Of course not!

LARRY

I am *not* –

ARLEN FINKLE

We don't make *moral* judgements!

106

LARRY

I went to the Aster Art *once*. I saw *Swedish Reverie*.

ARLEN FINKLE

It's okay, Larry, we don't need to know! The tenure
committee –

LARRY

It wasn't even erotic! Although it was, in a way.

ARLEN FINKLE

It's all right, Larry. Believe me.

Larry calms somewhat.

LARRY

. . . Okay.

ARLEN FINKLE

Okay. Okay. We, uh, we decide on Wednesday, so if there's
anything you want to submit in support of your tenure
application, we should have it by then. That's all.

LARRY

Submit. What? What do you –

ARLEN FINKLE

Well. Anything. Published work. Anything else you've done
outside of the institution. Any work that we might not be
aware of.

LARRY

I haven't done anything.

ARLEN FINKLE

Uh-huh.

LARRY

I haven't published.

ARLEN FINKLE

Uh-huh.

LARRY

Are you still getting those letters?

ARLEN FINKLE

Uh-huh.

LARRY

Those anonymous –

ARLEN FINKLE

Yes, I know. Yes.

A beat. Larry nods.

LARRY

Okay. Okay. Wednesday.

ARLEN FINKLE

Okay. Don't worry. Doing nothing is not bad. Ipso facto.
It's okay, relax. Try to relax.

MRS. SAMSKY'S BEDROOM

Larry is making strenuous love to Mrs. Samsky.

MRS. SAMSKY

So good . . . so good . . .

*She rolls on top of Larry to straddle him and, while humping, she
lights a mentholated cigarette. Larry moans.*

LARRY

Oh my God, Mrs Samsky . . .

*Above her head is the low cottage-cheese ceiling of the bedroom.
Outside we can hear Mr. Brandt mowing the lawn.*

We hear the front door opening.

Larry hisses:

. . . Who is it?

*Footsteps are approaching along the hall. Mrs. Samsky does not react;
her look, though uninvolved, stays on Larry even as the bedroom door
opens behind her and Clive Park enters wearing a traffic mask.*

Larry is mortified:

Clive, please! Wait outside!

Mrs. Samsky blows smoke into Larry's eyes.

Close on Larry as his eyes close against the smoke and then open again. A shadow falls across his face.

His point-of-view: a wooden plank is just being slid into place over his head to bring on black. The bang of hammer on nailhead. In the black:

> SY ABLEMAN'S VOICE
> Nailing it down is so impawtant.

We hear the chanting of kaddish and the sound of dirt hitting the top of the coffin. It drums a steady rhythm. Grace Slick's voice enters: "Somebody to Love". Another voice fills the break in the vocals just before the chorus:

> MRS. SAMSKY'S VOICE
> It's something we do. For recreation.

On the chorus downbeat, a crescent moon pops into the black. Mr. Brandt traverses the sky, pushing his lawnmower. A cow flies the opposite way. Stars twinkle. Sy Ableman walks across the sky dressed like a shtetl elder, a bindlestick over one shoulder.

Larry bolts upright in bed.

Sudden quiet.

Uncle Arthur is snoring in the tatty motel room's other bed.

A title:

MARSHAK

LARRY

He stands looking down in low shot. Overhead is cheap Johnson-Armstrong dropped ceiling.

> LARRY
> Please. I need help. I've already talked to the other rabbis. Please.

Reverse shows an elderly Eastern European woman seated behind a desk, looking up at Larry.

. . . I won't take much of his time. I need help. I need
Marshak. It's not about Danny's bar mitzvah. My boy
Danny. This coming shabbas. Very joyous event. That's all
fine. It's, it's more about myself, I've . . . I've had quite a bit
of *tsuris* lately. Marital problems. Professional. You name it.
This is not a frivolous request. This is a serious – I'm a
serious – I'm, uh, I've *tried* to be a serious man. You know,
tried to do right, be a member of the community, raise the,
raise the, Danny, Sarah, they both go to school, Hebrew
school, a good breakfast. Well, Danny goes to Hebrew
school, Sarah doesn't have time, she mostly . . . washes her
hair. Apparently there are several steps involved. But you
don't have to tell Marshak that. Just tell him I need help.
Please. I need help.

He lapses into silence, staring at the secretary.

She stares inscrutably back.

*After a moment she rises, goes to the door behind her, opens it, shuffles
into the dimness of an inner office decorated with arcana, Judaic and
otherwise.*

*Larry cranes to see past her. Her own body and the weak light
preclude a good view of the figure in the depths of the room. But one
can see that the man is old and bent, motionless behind a bare desk.*

Murmured voices in Hebrew.

Larry waits.

The murmuring ends.

*The old woman turns and shuffles back. She closes the door on the
motionless rabbi and sits creakily behind her own desk.*

SECRETARY

The rabbi is busy.

LARRY

He didn't look busy!

As she starts shuffling papers:

SECRETARY

He's thinking.

NIGHT

Larry, asleep in bed.

Weeping, soft, suppressed.

Larry stirs. He opens his eyes.

After a groggy beat he reacts to the weeping. He looks over.

LARRY

Arthur . . . ? Arthur?

Arthur is a dim mound on the next bed. His weeping continues.

For no reason Larry continues to keep his voice to a whisper:

. . . Arthur. What's wrong?

No answer.

. . . Arthur. It'll be okay. Arthur. We'll get Ron Meshbesher.
It'll be okay –

ARTHUR

AAAHHHH!

Shockingly loud, the scream is hard to interpret.

Arthur flings off his bedclothes, leaps from the bed and runs to the door. In boxer shorts and undershirt, he flings the door open and runs outside.

LARRY

Arthur!

Larry leaps from his bed, also in his underwear.

He goes to the door but pauses, peering cautiously out. Satisfied that the courtyard is deserted, he plunges into it.

COURTYARD

The courtyard/parking lot is hard lit by ghastly mercury vapor lights. The motel pool, surrounded by chain-link fence, has been drained. Its white concrete interior is cracked and weedy.

Uncle Arthur is hunched weeping in a corner of the pool enclosure.

LARRY

Arthur!

He opens the creaking gate and scurries over to Arthur.

. . . You've got to pull yourself together!

Arthur is suddenly angry. His voice slaps off the concrete:

ARTHUR

It's all shit, Larry! It's all shit!

LARRY

Arthur. Don't use that word.

ARTHUR

It's all fucking shit!

LARRY

Arthur! Come on!

ARTHUR

Look at everything *Hashem* has given you! And what do I get! I get fucking *shit*!

LARRY

Arthur. What do I have? I live at the Jolly Roger.

ARTHUR

You've got a *family*. You've got a *job*. *Hashem* hasn't given me *bupkes*.

LARRY

It's not fair to blame *Hashem*, Arthur. Please. Sometimes – please calm down – sometimes you have to help yourself.

ARTHUR

Don't blame me! You fucker!

LARRY

Arthur. Please.

ARTHUR

Hashem hasn't given me *shit*. Now I can't even play *cards*.

He resumes weeping.

LARRY

Arthur. This isn't the right forum. Please. Not by the pool.

Arthur weeps.

Arthur . . . It's okay . . . It's okay . . .

MORNING

Larry and Arthur are driving. In the windshield through which we look at them, the reflections of towering conifers stream by. It seems to be a glorious day.

LARRY

Is this it?

Both men peer out.

ARTHUR

I think so . . . yeah . . . there . . .

He nods at the road ahead.

A signpost, the old-fashioned kind with wooden fingers pointing the different directions, has one finger indicating the way to "Canada".

We tip off the sign as Larry's car passes and recedes. There is a canoe strapped to its roof.

BOUNDARY WATERS

Beautiful, wooded, remote.

The car is parked at water's edge, having backed down a two-track lane worn through the undergrowth. Larry and Arthur are lowering their canoe into the water.

LARRY

Okay . . .

He straightens. Arthur straightens. Larry hugs him.

. . . Look . . .

They separate and Larry pulls a white envelope from his pocket and gives it to Arthur.

. . . This'll help you get back on your feet.

Arthur looks into the envelope.

ARTHUR
Oh my God. Where did you get this?

LARRY
Doesn't matter. When you –

ARTHUR
This is a lot of money!

LARRY
It should get you started.

ARTHUR
This is a lot of money! Are you sure you don't need it?

LARRY
Arthur, I'm fine. Come on, get in. When you're settled . . .

Arthur climbs into the canoe.

. . . let me know how to get in touch.

He pushes the boat off. Arthur twists to look back. As he drifts away:

ARTHUR
Are you sure this is okay?

LARRY
It's fine. It's fine.

Larry waves.

Arthur waves bravely back, then turns to pick up the paddle. A couple of strokes and he turns back with a last thought.

ARTHUR
Larry. I'm sorry. What I said last night.

LARRY
I know. It's okay.

A lingering look from Arthur, and then he turns back to paddle.

A gunshot.

Blood spurts from the back of Uncle Arthur's neck.

He slumps forward, dead.

VOICE

Good shot!

Larry looks wildly around. He sees:

Mr. Brandt and Mitch in their camo fatigues, hard to pick out in the foliage. They are looking toward the canoe, Mitch just lowering his rifle.

Mr. Brandt's look swings into the lens. He points at us:

. . . There's another Jew, son.

Mitch swings his rifle up at us.

He fires.

LARRY

Gasping awake in the motel room.

He looks around.

It is dawn.

Arthur sits on the edge of his bed in his underwear, staring slackjawed into space, vacant-eyed, drained.

Larry gazes around the room, waiting for things to fall into place.

Finally, blearily:

LARRY

Were we . . . out at the pool last night?

Arthur responds in a flat, empty voice:

ARTHUR

Yes. I'm sorry.

Larry blinks sleep away.

After a beat:

> LARRY
>
> It's shabbas.

Another beat.

Arthur heaves a deep sigh.

> ARTHUR
>
> I'll go drain my cyst.

RESTROOM

Day. A two-urinal, two-stall men's room of old tile and yellowed fixtures.

We are low. One of the stall doors is closed. Under it we see the dress shoes and dress-pant cuffs of two young men standing inside.

We hear a long sucking inhale.

> RONNIE NUDELL'S VOICE
>
> Gimme that fucker.

A loudly projected echoing male voice:

> VOICE
>
> Ya'amod habrayshit.

SANCTUARY

Danny, seated in the front pew with his parents and sister and Uncle Arthur, rises and walks along the lip of the bema. His eyes are wide and red-rimmed.

The prelapped voice was his call to the Torah. All eyes in the congregation, which fills the large sanctuary, are on him.

In great echoing silence he walks to the steps on the right side of the bema and climbs.

The right-side lectern is surrounded by a gaggle of old Jewish men.

They busy themselves with the preparation of the pair of scrolls resting on the lectern, rolling them, pausing, rolling some more, muttering prayers, kissing the scrolls by means of their tsitsit. *They pay Danny no attention.*

Danny takes his place centered behind the lectern. His chin comes up to the bottom of the reading platform.

Men continue to mutter prayers around him. A pair of hands appears on his shoulders from behind. Danny looks down at the strange hands. They pull him back.

A foot drags a small riser out from under the lectern.

Hands push Danny up onto the riser.

We boom up on the Torah scrolls, still being busily rolled.

Beyond it, a sea of faces.

The yad – *a molded tin pointer – is thrust into Danny's hand. The non-pointing end has a red silken tassel.*

Danny looks at the bouncing tassel. He looks at the little pointing finger, the business end of the yad.

Men mutter around him, each a different prayer. They dip and doven.

Danny watches as his own hand points the yad *down at the scroll.*

The scroll is a swarm of Hebrew letters. Danny squints.

One voice separates from the murmurs around him. It chants, insistently, in a sotto-voce falsetto:

> VOICE
> Vayidaber adonai al Moshe b'har Sinai laymor . . .

Danny stares at the end of the yad *against the parchment scroll.*

Someone's hand enters and moves the yad *to the correct spot in the text.*

The prompting voice again:

> . . . Vayidaber adonai al Moshe b'har Sinai laymor . . .

Danny looks up from the scrolls.

In the congregation Ronnie Nudell sits squished between his parents. He returns Danny's red-rimmed slackjawed stare.

The insistent voice:

... Vayidaber adonai al Moshe b'har Sinai laymor ...

Danny looks over.

From the surrounding scrum the prompter nods at him. He looks somewhat like Cantor Youssele Rosenblatt.

... Vayidaber adonai al Moshe b'har Sinai laymor ...

Danny looks back down at the scroll. A hand enters to tap a pointing finger where the yad *points.*

... Vayidaber adonai al Moshe b'har Si –

Danny erupts:

DANNY
Vayidaber adonai al Moshe b'har Sinai laymor ...

PROMPTER
Mm-hm.

Danny continues to boom out the Torah portion, tracking the yad *along the line of text.*

In the congregation, Larry and Judith watch. We hear Danny chanting fluently and Larry squeezes the hand Judith has laced through his arm.

Judith whispers:

JUDITH
I'm sorry that ... things have been so hard for us ...

LARRY
It's okay.

JUDITH
Sy had so much respect for you, Larry.

He pats her hand.

A beat.

... He wrote letters to the tenure committee.

LATER

The congregation is loudly singing V'Zos Hatorah. *Danny is now seated in a highbacked chair upstage on the bema.*

His point-of-view: a tallised man of late middle age hoists the open scroll off the lectern and turns as he raises the Torah high to display it. The man is sweating. The heavy scrolls vibrate with his effort to keep them aloft. As the congregation continues to sing we hear him mutter:

MAN

Jesus Christ . . .

LATER

Danny stands at the lectern facing Rabbi Nachtner who holds out to him a small kiddush cup.

Although Rabbi Nachtner seems to be addressing Danny, he is projecting loudly.

NACHTNER

. . . taking your place as a member of our tribe. You will go and see Rabbi Marshak after the service. You will celebrate in a reception downstairs in Schanfield Hall. And then you will be a member of B'Nai Abraham and of the Nation of Israel. Danny Gopnik, the Sisterhood makes a gift to you of this kiddush cup so that you will remember this blessed day on the next shabbas and the next, and on every shabbas of a long and fruitful life, and, until that wonderful day when you stand under the *chupa*, we say . . .

CONGREGATION

Amen.

Danny, still red-eyed, tries to focus.

His point-of-view shows the kiddush cup large in the foreground, extended by the beaming rabbi.

His own hand rises into frame to grasp the cup.

The congregation starts Adon Olam.

A DOOR

Creaking open. The cut has snapped off the robust Adon Olam, *leaving sepulchral quiet.*

Danny, clutching his kiddush cup, hesitantly enters the dim study. Marshak's elderly Eastern European gatekeeper closes the door behind him.

Marshak is an old man staring at him from behind a bare desktop. His look, eyes magnified by thick glasses, is impossible to read.

Danny creeps to the chair facing the desk. He gingerly sits on the squeaking leather upholstery, self-conscious under Marshak's stare.

Marshak's slow, regular, phlegmy mouth-breathing is the only sound in the room.

A long beat. The two stare at each other.

Marshak smacks his lips a couple of times, wetting surfaces in preparation for speach.

Another beat.

Finally:

> MARSHAK
> When the truth is found. To be lies.

He pauses. He clears his throat.

At length:

> . . . And all the hope. Within you dies.

Another beat. Danny waits. Marshak stares.

He smacks his lips again. He thinks.

> . . . Then what?

Danny doesn't answer. It is unclear whether answer is expected.

Quiet.

Marshak clears his throat with a loud and thorough hawking.

The hawking abates. Marshak sniffs.

. . . Grace Slick. Marty Balin. Paul Kanta. Jorma . . .
somethin'. These are the membas of the Airplane.

He nods a couple of times.

. . . Interesting.

*He reaches up and slowly opens his desk drawer. He withdraws
something. He lays it on the bare desk and pushes it across.*

. . . . Here.

It is Danny's radio.

. . . Be a good boy.

LARRY'S OFFICE

Larry is at his desk, sorting through mail.

ARLEN FINKLE
(*off*)
Danny was magnificent.

*Larry looks up: Arlen leans in his accustomed spot in the office
doorway.*

LARRY
Oh. Thank you, Arlen.

ARLEN FINKLE
Mazel tov. It was wonderful.

LARRY
Yes it was. Thank you.

ARLEN FINKLE
Such a time of *nachas*, Larry. He's your youngest. You have
to savor it.

LARRY
I do. I will.

ARLEN FINKLE
See you at the staff caf.

                              LARRY
   Yes.

Arlen shoves off to go, but hesitates.

                          ARLEN FINKLE
   I just . . . I shouldn't tell you. I'm not telling you officially.
   The tenure candidates aren't notified till Monday.

                              LARRY
   . . . Yes?

Arlen nods.

                          ARLEN FINKLE
   You'll be very pleased.

Larry stares at him.

                              LARRY
   Thank you, Arlen.

Arlen goes, calling without looking back:

                          ARLEN FINKLE
   I didn't say anything. Mazel tov.

HEBREW SCHOOL CORRIDOR

Distant thunder at the cut.

*We are tracking behind Marshak's tea lady as she shuffles down the
hall, clutching a stack of papers.*

LARRY'S OFFICE

Mail in front of him.

He opens an envelope: from "Ronald Meshbesher, Esq."

In it is a letter headed: "Retainer Agreement."

Underneath is an invoice. The amount: $3,000.

Arriving rain begins to patter at the window.

HEBREW SCHOOL CLASS

The teacher leads the class in drill.

Danny has a book tilted toward him on his desktop. It once again hides his radio, the earpiece of which is once again in his ear.

The door opens and the tea lady shuffles to the teacher. She hands him a sheet from off her stack.

The teacher puts on reading glasses and inspects it. As he reads, thunder crashes, closer.

LARRY'S OFFICE

He fingers the invoice.

Close on a printed detail, "Payable", and, typed underneath: "Upon Receipt".

Wind whips rain against the window.

HEBREW SCHOOL CLASS

The teacher taps the desktop for attention.

> TEACHER
> *Chaverim*, there's a tornado warning from the weather service. Rabbi Marshak has decided to move us over to the basement of the shul . . .

Hubbub in the classrooom.

> . . . *Sheket. Sheket.* We're gonna form two lines. This is orderly. *Hakol b'seder.*

LARRY'S OFFICE

He stares down at his desktop.

Thunder.

He reaches up and scratches his nose, staring.

On the desk: a ledger sheet with a list of students' names. Next to each name, a grade.

Larry drums his fingers.

He picks up a pencil.

He goes down to "Park, Clive". Next to it is an F.

He waggles the pencil, eraser-end thumping the sheet.

He erases the "F". He enters a "C".

The pencil leaves frame. We hold on the new grade.

After a beat the hand re-enters to put a minus sign after the "C".

The hand withdraws.

The phone jangles, harshly.

Larry looks at it, frozen.

He lets it ring a couple times.

He reaches for it. He hesitantly unprongs it.

> LARRY

. . . Hello?

> VOICE

Larry?

> LARRY

. . . Yes?

> VOICE

Hi, Len Shapiro.

> LARRY

Oh. Hello, Dr. Shapiro.

> DR. SHAPIRO

Listen, mazel tov on Danny.

> LARRY

Yes, thank you.

> DR. SHAPIRO

Listen, could you come in to discuss these X-ray results?

Larry sits frozen, phone to his ear.

. . . Hello?

> LARRY
> Yes?

> DR. SHAPIRO
> Larry, could you come in and discuss these X-ray results? Remember the X-rays we took?

> LARRY
> . . . We can't discuss them on the phone?

Thunder. Pattering rain.

> DR. SHAPIRO
> I think we'd be more comfortable in person. Can you come in?

A beat.

> LARRY
> When?

> DR. SHAPIRO
> Now. Now is good. I've cleared some time now.

TALMUD TORAH PARKING LOT

It is overcast, dark, and extremely windy. The students mill about in flapping clothes, Danny with his radio earpiece still in place.

A teacher is fumbling with keys at the door to the shul.

Mark Sallerson shouts above the wind:

> MARK SALLERSON
> That fucking flag is gonna rip right off the flagpole!

CAR

We are looking at Larry through a windshield lashed by rain. He drives with hands clenched on the wheel. Wipers pump to keep up with the rain. The cars behind have their lights on. It has gotten quite dark.

Passing street lights rhythmically sweep Larry's face, their light stippled and bent by the rain on the windows.

TALMUD TORAH PARKING LOT

Danny's head bobs in time to the music. Wind whips his hair. We hear, very compressed, the beginning of "Somebody to Love".

Danny spots a shaggy-haired youth among the milling students.

DANNY

Hey! Fagle!

Danny notices something past Fagle: a funnel cloud in the middle distance.

A growing rumble. The tornado is approaching.

At the first downbeat of its chorus the Jefferson Airplane song bumps up full.

We cut to black, and credits.

NEW PLAYS

★ **AS BEES IN HONEY DROWN by Douglas Carter Beane.** Winner of the John Gassner Playwriting Award. A hot young novelist finds the subject of his new screenplay in a New York socialite who leads him into the world of *Auntie Mame* and *Breakfast at Tiffany's*, before she takes him for a ride. "A delicious soufflé of a satire … [an] extremely entertaining fable for an age that always chooses image over substance." *–The NY Times* "… A witty assessment of one of the most active and relentless industries in a consumer society … the creation of 'hot' young things, which the media have learned to mass produce with efficiency and zeal." *–The NY Daily News* [3M, 3W, flexible casting] ISBN: 0-8222-1651-5

★ **STUPID KIDS by John C. Russell.** In rapid, highly stylized scenes, the story follows four high-school students as they make their way from first through eighth period and beyond, struggling with the fears, frustrations, and longings peculiar to youth. "In STUPID KIDS … playwright John C. Russell gets the opera of adolescence to a T … The stylized teenspeak of STUPID KIDS … suggests that Mr. Russell may have hidden a tape recorder under a desk in study hall somewhere and then scoured the tapes for good quotations … it is the kids' insular, ceaselessly churning world, a pre-adult world of Doritos and libidos, that the playwright seeks to lay bare." *–The NY Times* "STUPID KIDS [is] a sharp-edged … whoosh of teen angst and conformity anguish. It is also very funny." *–NY Newsday* [2M, 2W] ISBN: 0-8222-1698-1

★ **COLLECTED STORIES by Donald Margulies.** From Obie Award-winner Donald Margulies comes a provocative analysis of a student-teacher relationship that turns sour when the protégé becomes a rival. "With his fine ear for detail, Margulies creates an authentic, insular world, and he gives equal weight to the opposing viewpoints of two formidable characters." *–The LA Times* "This is probably Margulies' best play to date …" *–The NY Post* "… always fluid and lively, the play is thick with ideas, like a stock-pot of good stew." *–The Village Voice* [2W] ISBN: 0-8222-1640-X

★ **FREEDOMLAND by Amy Freed.** An overdue showdown between a son and his father sets off fireworks that illuminate the neurosis, rage and anxiety of one family – and of America at the turn of the millennium. "FREEDOMLAND's more obvious links are to *Buried Child* and *Bosoms and Neglect*. Freed, like Guare, is an inspired wordsmith with a gift for surreal touches in situations grounded in familiar and real territory." *–Curtain Up* [3M, 4W] ISBN: 0-8222-1719-8

★ **STOP KISS by Diana Son.** A poignant and funny play about the ways, both sudden and slow, that lives can change irrevocably. "There's so much that is vital and exciting about STOP KISS … you want to embrace this young author and cheer her onto other works … the writing on display here is funny and credible … you also will be charmed by its heartfelt characters and up-to-the-minute humor." *–The NY Daily News* "… irresistibly exciting … a sweet, sad, and enchantingly sincere play." *–The NY Times* [3M, 3W] ISBN: 0-8222-1731-7

★ **THREE DAYS OF RAIN by Richard Greenberg.** The sins of fathers and mothers make for a bittersweet elegy in this poignant and revealing drama. "… a work so perfectly judged it heralds the arrival of a major playwright … Greenberg is extraordinary." *–The NY Daily News* "Greenberg's play is filled with graceful passages that are by turns melancholy, harrowing, and often, quite funny." *–Variety* [2M, 1W] ISBN: 0-8222-1676-0

★ **THE WEIR by Conor McPherson.** In a bar in rural Ireland, the local men swap spooky stories in an attempt to impress a young woman from Dublin who recently moved into a nearby "haunted" house. However, the tables are soon turned when she spins a yarn of her own. "You shed all sense of time at this beautiful and devious new play." *–The NY Times* "Sheer theatrical magic. I have rarely been so convinced that I have just seen a modern classic. Tremendous." *–The London Daily Telegraph* [4M, 1W] ISBN: 0-8222-1706-6

DRAMATISTS PLAY SERVICE, INC.
440 Park Avenue South, New York, NY 10016 212-683-8960 Fax 212-213-1539
postmaster@dramatists.com www.dramatists.com

SOUND EFFECTS

Music and laughter of a party
People counting down to the New Year
People singing "Auld Lang Syne"
Sounds of a dance
Band playing a tarantella
Shouts